The Last Kingdom

The Last Kingdom

A Journey into the Kingdom That Lasts Forever

STEVEN E. GOODENOUGH

WIPF & STOCK · Eugene, Oregon

THE LAST KINGDOM
A Journey into the Kingdom That Lasts Forever

Copyright © 2025 Steven E. Goodenough. All rights reserved. Except for brief quotations in critical publications or reviews, no part of this book may be reproduced in any manner without prior written permission from the publisher. Write: Permissions, Wipf and Stock Publishers, 199 W. 8th Ave., Suite 3, Eugene, OR 97401.

Wipf & Stock
An Imprint of Wipf and Stock Publishers
199 W. 8th Ave., Suite 3
Eugene, OR 97401

www.wipfandstock.com

PAPERBACK ISBN: 979-8-3852-4142-2
HARDCOVER ISBN: 979-8-3852-4143-9
EBOOK ISBN: 979-8-3852-4144-6

All Scripture quotations, unless otherwise indicated, are taken from the Holy Bible, New International Version®, NIV®. Copyright ©1973, 1978, 1984, 2011 by Biblica, Inc.™ Used by permission of Zondervan. All rights reserved worldwide. www.zondervan.com. The "NIV" and "New International Version" are trademarks registered in the United States Patent and Trademark Office by Biblica, Inc.™

Scripture quotations taken from the (NASB®) New American Standard Bible®, Copyright © 1960, 1971, 1977, 1995, 2020 by The Lockman Foundation. Used by permission. All rights reserved. lockman.org

Contents

Preface ix

Introduction: The Last Kingdom 1

Chapter 1: The Gospel 3
    The Meaning of the Gospel 3
    Jesus's Proclamation of the Gospel 4
    The Sermon on the Mount: Training for Kingdom Living 4
    The Good News vs. Religious Legalism 4
    The Centurion's Great Faith 5
    Faith and Works: A Kingdom Balance 6
    The Power of Repentance: Personal and Communal Transformation 6
    The Cost of Rejection: Understanding Judgment and God's Response 7
    Conclusion 7
    Chapter 1 Study Questions 8

Chapter 2: The Power of God for Salvation 10
    The Gospel: God's Power for Deliverance 10
    The Wrath of God: Understanding Paul's Message 10
    Historical Influences on the Concept of Wrath 11
    God's Character Revealed Through Jesus 12
    The Meaning of Propitiation: Active Grace, Not Appeasement 13
    God's Plan of Reconciliation Through Christ 13
    The Judgment of Unbelief 13

Contents

Romans 1:18 and God's Wrath as Separation 14
The Consequences of Rejecting God's Grace 15
Conclusion 16
Chapter 2 Study Questions 16

Chapter 3: The Kingdom of God 19
    Understanding the Kingdom of God 19
    Heavenly and Earthly Kingdoms 19
    The Spiritual Nature of the Kingdom of God 20
    Prophetic Glimpses of the Kingdom in the Old Testament 21
    The Eternal Kingdom: God's Reign Through Christ 21
    Believers as Ambassadors of the Kingdom 22
    The Future Physical Kingdom 22
    The Present Yet Future Reality of the Kingdom 23
    Conclusion 24
    Chapter 3 Study Questions 25

Chapter 4: Kingdom Citizens 27
    A New Identity in Christ: From Slaves to Heirs 28
    Jesus as Our Kinsman-Redeemer 29
    Seated with Christ: A New Position of Authority 29
    Unity and Service in the Kingdom 30
    Maturing as Citizens of the Kingdom 31
    Conclusion 32
    Chapter 4 Study Questions 33

Chapter 5: Citizens with a Purpose 35
    Renewing the Mind 35
    Paul's Prayer for Enlightenment 36
    Spiritual Blessings in Christ 36
    Chosen and Adopted in Love 36
    Redemption Through Christ's Blood 38
    Revealing the Mystery of God's Will 38
    God's Administration: *Oikonomia* 39
    Sealed with the Holy Spirit 39
    Experiencing the Power of God 40
    Living by the Spirit's Power 40

Conclusion 42
Chapter 5 Study Questions 42

Chapter 6: Overcoming Obstacles to Spiritual Maturity 45
   Identifying Spiritual Obstacles 45
   Cultural Pressures Then and Now 46
   Living Out Our Faith in Practice 47
   Pulling Down Strongholds 49
   Put On the Armor of God 50
   Conclusion 51
   Chapter 6 Study Questions 52

Chapter 7: Renewing the Mind 54
   A Life of Devotion and Transformation 54
   Humility, Unity, and Love in Action 55
      Verses 3–8: Humility and Unity in Diversity
      Verses 9–13: Love and Service in Action
      Verses 14–21: Responding to Opposition with Grace
   Application for Renewing the Mind 56
   Understanding Discipline in Scripture 58
   Steps for a Renewed Mind: Joy, Prayer, and Gratitude 59
      Rejoice Always
      Pray Continually
      Give Thanks in All Circumstances
   Living as Ambassadors for Christ 61
   Chapter 7 Study Questions 62

Chapter 8: The Gospel in a Digital Age 64
   Navigating Distractions and Staying Authentic 64
   Prophetic Insights for a Connected World 66
   The Digital Age as Iron Mixed with Clay 66
   A World Under Control 67
   A Global Witness and Influence 67
   Living with Integrity and Kingdom Focus 68
   Guarding Against Compromise 68
   Security in God's Promise 69
   Focusing on the Eternal Kingdom 69

Contents

A Life Set Apart 70
Paul's Call to Live Differently 70
A Hardened Heart and Lost Sensitivity 70
A Renewed Life in Christ 71
Transformed by the Gospel 72
Guarding Our Minds with Intentional Focus 72
Conclusion 73
Chapter 8 Study Questions 74

Chapter 9: The Unshakable Kingdom: Living with Hope and Purpose 76
    A Kingdom That Will Not Fade 76
    Reflecting on Our Journey 76
    Living as Citizens in the Present Age 78
    The Question of Suffering 80
    God's Plan of Restoration Through Christ 80
    The Battle Against God's Design 80
    A Purpose in Allowing Free Will 81
    The Purpose of Suffering 82
    Our Present Sufferings and Future Glory 83
    The Coming of God's Kingdom 83
    The Kingdom Among Us 84
    The Parable of the Mustard Seed 84
    A Call to Align with God's Will 84
    The Spread of the Gospel and the Kingdom's Fulfillment 85
    An Inheritance of Eternal Kingdom 85
    Living with Eternal Purpose 85
    Living as Citizens of an Unshakable Kingdom 86
    Conclusion 87
    Chapter 9 Study Questions 88

Chapter 10: Embracing the Kingdom Life 90
    Chapter 10 Study Questions 91

Glossary of Key Terms 95

Bibliography 101

Preface

THE JOURNEY TO WRITING *The Last Kingdom* has been one of discovery, growth, and deep reflection. This book was born out of a personal quest to understand what it truly means to live as a citizen of God's Kingdom in a world often at odds with his design. It is both a response to the cultural challenges we face and an invitation to embrace the unshakable hope, purpose, and identity found in Christ.

In today's fast-paced and digitally driven age, the call to live with a Kingdom mindset is more pressing than ever. We are constantly bombarded by messages that seek to define our worth, shape our priorities, and draw our attention away from what truly matters. Yet, amidst the noise, God's Word remains a steadfast guide, offering timeless truths for navigating these complexities and anchoring our lives in his eternal purposes.

Throughout this book, you will find a blend of scriptural exploration, practical application, and personal insights. My aim is to take you on a journey that not only deepens your understanding of God's Kingdom but also equips you to live it out in your daily life. Together, we will explore themes of identity, transformation, spiritual maturity, and the hope of the eternal Kingdom to come.

As you read, I encourage you to approach this book not just as a study of theological concepts but as an opportunity to reflect on your own journey. Each chapter is designed to challenge and inspire, prompting you to consider how God is calling you to align your life with his Kingdom. My prayer is that this book will serve

Preface

as a catalyst for growth, empowering you to live with clarity, purpose, and confidence in who you are as a child of God.

The Kingdom of God is not merely a future reality; it is a present truth with profound implications for how we live, think, and engage with the world around us. As Jesus declared, "The kingdom of God has come near. Repent and believe the good news!" (Mark 1:15). This declaration invites us to step into a new reality, one that transforms our perspective and compels us to reflect his light in a darkened world.

I am deeply grateful to those who have walked alongside me in this journey—my family, friends, mentors, and readers who have encouraged and sharpened my understanding of Kingdom living. Your support has been a vital part of this work, and I pray that this book will honor the faithfulness you have shown.

May *The Last Kingdom* inspire you to pursue the life God has called you to live, a life marked by integrity, hope, and unwavering devotion to his truth. As you turn these pages, I pray that the words within will resonate with your heart, drawing you closer to the King and his eternal Kingdom.

In his grace,

Steven E. Goodenough

Introduction: The Last Kingdom

WE LIVE IN A world filled with countless kingdoms—nations, cultures, corporations, ideologies—all competing for influence, power, and loyalty. Amidst all this noise and shifting power, there exists a different kind of kingdom. A kingdom that stands above them all. It's the Kingdom of God. This isn't just another lofty idea or abstract belief—it's a reality with the power to transform everything you thought you knew about life, identity, and purpose.

The Last Kingdom invites you to journey into this kingdom—the one Jesus proclaimed, embodied, and calls each of us into. But be warned: this journey isn't for the fainthearted. It's not about following religious rules, aligning with any human agenda, or seeking self-improvement for its own sake. It's an invitation to leave behind the familiar and step into a new way of life that redefines how you see yourself, the world, and your purpose. You're not just learning about a distant heaven; you're stepping into a calling to live as a citizen of a kingdom that challenges every value and expectation the world holds dear.

What if the message of God's kingdom isn't just good news—it's the best news, redefining who you are and what you're here for? Imagine discovering a life where true freedom, purpose, and belonging are yours—not in some far-off hope, but here and now as we embrace the reality of God's reign. *The Last Kingdom* will reveal what it means to live in this kingdom today, how it enables us to shed the world's empty pursuits, and why it's the only kingdom that will truly endure.

As you turn these pages, we'll dig deep into the gospel, uncovering why repentance is essential—not just a one-time decision, but a continual turning toward God that reshapes our minds, hearts, and actions. This journey is about living with the assurance that God's kingdom isn't only coming but is already here, breaking through into our lives and reshaping the world around us.

If you're ready to go beyond surface-level faith, to ask the hard questions, and to discover a life anchored in God's eternal Kingdom, *The Last Kingdom* is here to guide you. Together, we'll unlock the mystery, power, and purpose of God's kingdom—a kingdom whose King is unlike any other, whose values defy the world's, and whose message holds the key to the life you were made for. This journey promises not just understanding but transformation—a way of life that brings wholeness, purpose, and joy in ways the world cannot give.

Are you ready to step into *The Last Kingdom* and live the life you were made for?

CHAPTER 1

The Gospel

THE MEANING OF THE GOSPEL

THE WORD "GOSPEL" COMES from the Greek *evangelion* (*ev-an-gel-ee-on*), which means "good news" or "glad tidings." It's about proclaiming something transformative that brings joy and purpose. Imagine you've inherited a vast fortune. Just before you risk squandering it, you discover that part of your inheritance includes expert guidance to help you think and act like someone capable of managing wealth responsibly. The gospel offers something far greater, yet similar—it's an invitation to live in a new reality, with Christ's teachings and the Spirit's help as our guide.

John the Baptist was the first to announce this good news. His message was simple yet powerful: "Repent, for the kingdom of heaven is at hand" (Matt 3:2). Repentance means turning around and going in a new direction, not only in actions but in mindset and beliefs. It's more than changing outward behaviors; it involves a deep internal shift in how we view God and ourselves. John's message set the stage for Jesus, calling people to leave old ways of thinking and embrace a new perspective on life and eternity.

JESUS'S PROCLAMATION OF THE GOSPEL

After Jesus completed forty days of fasting and facing temptation in the wilderness, he began his ministry with the same call: "Repent, for the kingdom of heaven is at hand" (Matt 4:17). Jesus then traveled throughout Galilee, teaching in synagogues and proclaiming the gospel of the kingdom (Matt 4:23). This gospel wasn't merely about personal salvation. It was an announcement of God's kingdom breaking into the world—a challenge to old thinking and an invitation into a new reality.

THE SERMON ON THE MOUNT: TRAINING FOR KINGDOM LIVING

In Matt 5, we read that Jesus went up on a mountain, sat down, and began teaching his disciples. This teaching, known as the Sermon on the Mount (Matt 5:1—7:27), was revolutionary. Many people view the Sermon as a set of moral lessons—"Do this, and you'll get that"—but Jesus's message is much more profound. Just like the expert who guides an inheritor to manage wealth, Jesus taught his followers how to live as members of God's kingdom. His focus wasn't on rules to gain entrance; he was describing the mindset and character of those who already belong. Kingdom living is rooted in who we are, not just in what we do.

THE GOOD NEWS VS. RELIGIOUS LEGALISM

The good news of the kingdom was radical. It contradicted much of what people thought was required to be right with God. The religious leaders emphasized strict adherence to man-made traditions and interpretations of the law, believing that outward conformity was the way to please God. But Jesus turned this thinking on its head. Entering the kingdom doesn't come through ritual or tradition—it's about repentance and a transformed heart. This transformation is not an external process but an internal one, reshaping our minds and hearts according to God's design.

THE CENTURION'S GREAT FAITH

One of the most powerful examples of this transformation is the story of the centurion who came to Jesus in Capernaum (Matt 8:5–11). The centurion's servant was paralyzed and suffering terribly, and when Jesus offered to come and heal him, the centurion responded with remarkable faith: "Lord, I am not worthy for You to come under my roof; just say the word, and my servant will be healed" (Matt 8:8). Jesus marveled at his faith, saying, "I have not found such great faith with anyone in Israel" (Matt 8:10). The centurion's trust in Jesus wasn't based on tradition or law but on a shift in his beliefs. He accepted Jesus's authority, showing that entering the kingdom is about a heart transformed by faith, not adhering to rules.

Similarly, the story of the rich young ruler reveals that outward obedience isn't enough without a transformed heart (Matt 19:16–22). In this account, a young man approaches Jesus, wanting to know how he can inherit eternal life. He's kept the commandments since his youth and believes he's doing everything right. Jesus sees his sincerity but also knows there's something holding him back. So he tells him, "Go, sell your possessions and give to the poor, and you will have treasure in heaven. Then come, follow me."

At this, the young man's true priorities come to light. Though he's followed the commandments, his heart is tied to his wealth. When Jesus asks him to give it up, he walks away grieving, unable to part with his treasure. Outward obedience can look impressive, but it can mask deeper attachments. Despite all his efforts, he wasn't fully surrendered to God. His story reminds us that transformation goes beyond surface-level faith and calls for a deeper, inner shift that reorders our loves and loyalties, placing God above all else. Outward obedience cannot replace the internal transformation of the heart.

FAITH AND WORKS: A KINGDOM BALANCE

The message of the kingdom is clear: we are saved by grace through faith, not by works (Eph 2:8–9). Salvation is a gift from God, not something we can earn. However, true faith is never passive; it always leads to action. Just as faith leads to good works, it also leads to repentance. Faith and belief come from the same root word, but they function differently. Belief is a noun—it's what you hold to be true. Faith, however, is a verb—it's about action. Your actions will always reflect what you truly believe. As James says, "Faith by itself, if it is not accompanied by action, is dead" (Jas 2:17).

Think of faith and works as two sides of the same coin. Faith in Jesus transforms us from the inside out, and good works naturally follow—acts of love, justice, mercy, and service. These works don't earn a place in the kingdom; they are evidence of belonging. Jesus said, "You will know them by their fruits" (Matt 7:16). The fruit of our lives shows the world that we belong to the kingdom. Ephesians 2:10 reinforces this: "For we are God's workmanship, created in Christ Jesus to do good works, which God prepared in advance for us to do." We aren't saved by good works, but we are saved for good works.

THE POWER OF REPENTANCE: PERSONAL AND COMMUNAL TRANSFORMATION

Repentance is more than feeling sorry; it's about turning back to God's design and purpose for our lives. When we realign with his design, it doesn't just impact us personally—it can transform our relationships, communities, and even society as a whole. But for true repentance to happen, we first need to understand what's keeping us from living in that alignment. This is where we confront the reality of sin. I define sin as functioning outside of God's design and purpose. The Greek word *hamartia* (hah-mar-TEE-ah) means "missing the mark," which isn't just about breaking rules; it's about falling short of the life God intended for us.

Think of it like trying to fix something with the wrong tool. You wouldn't use a screwdriver to hammer a nail; it would be frustrating and damaging. Likewise, when we operate outside God's design, we cannot live as he intended, leading to brokenness within ourselves and in our communities.

This is why repentance is so powerful. It's not merely about forgiveness; it's about realigning with God's original plan. When Jesus and John the Baptist preached repentance, they called people to return to God's design, individually and as a community. Repentance can shift our focus toward love, justice, and mercy.

Consider Zacchaeus. He didn't just apologize for cheating people; he made restitution, impacting his entire community (Luke 19:8). True repentance changes us, and it also changes the world around us, restoring what was broken and bringing us back in line with God's perfect design.

THE COST OF REJECTION: UNDERSTANDING JUDGMENT AND GOD'S RESPONSE

Despite witnessing miracles and hearing the good news, many cities did not repent (Matt 11:20-24). If God desires everyone to repent, why do some people still reject him? The Bible shows that God's judgment respects free will. John 3:19-21 says, "This is the judgment, that the Light has come into the world, and men loved the darkness rather than the Light" (John 3:19). Judgment here isn't about God forcing a decision; it's about allowing people the freedom to choose, even if it means separation from him.

Jesus's warnings weren't scare tactics. They revealed the reality of choosing to walk away from God. God doesn't force anyone into the kingdom—he honors our choices.

CONCLUSION

The gospel is the good news of the kingdom of heaven, announcing its arrival and calling for repentance. It's not about obeying religious laws but about a heart and mind transformed by faith. We are saved by grace, and true faith will naturally lead to action. Repentance aligns us with God's design, impacting both our lives and the world around us. God's judgment isn't forced on anyone—it's the result of choices, as God honors our free will. How we respond to the gospel matters not only for our relationship with God but for how we live, serve, and impact the world around us.

CHAPTER 1 STUDY QUESTIONS

1. **Understanding the Gospel:** How would you explain the concept of the gospel as "good news" in your own words? What makes it "good" for you personally, and how does it impact your life?

2. **Repentance and Transformation:** The gospel calls us to "repent," which means changing direction in mindset and behavior. What are some areas of life where you feel a need to shift perspective or actions to align more with God's design?

3. **Jesus's Teachings on Kingdom Living:** Reflecting on the Sermon on the Mount, how do you see Jesus's teachings as a guide for living as a part of God's kingdom? Are there any particular principles from the Sermon that resonate with you or challenge you?

4. **Faith in Action:** The chapter emphasizes that true faith leads to action. What are some practical ways you can express your faith through actions that reflect kingdom values? How do you balance faith and works in your own life?

5. **Repentance Beyond Personal Transformation:** Repentance has the potential to impact not just individual lives but also communities. What does this look like in practice? How can our personal alignment with God's design contribute to positive change around us?

6. **Judgment and Free Will:** This chapter describes God's judgment as respecting free will, where rejection of the gospel is

honored. How do you interpret this concept of judgment, and how does it shape your view of God's character?

7. **Living in the New Reality of the Kingdom:** The gospel invites us to live in a new reality with Jesus as our guide. What challenges or obstacles do you encounter when trying to live out this kingdom reality in your daily life? How might you overcome them?

CHAPTER 2

The Power of God for Salvation

THE GOSPEL: GOD'S POWER FOR DELIVERANCE

THE APOSTLE PAUL BOLDLY declares in Rom 1:16–17 that the gospel is "the power of God for salvation to everyone who believes" (author's paraphrase). The Greek word for salvation, *soteria*, means deliverance. A more literal translation would read, "The gospel is the power of God for deliverance to everyone who believes." But deliverance from what? To fully grasp the true power of the gospel, we need to understand what Paul and the early Christians meant by deliverance and why this concept was so central to their message.

This deliverance can mean many things—freedom from sin, restoration of our relationship with God, spiritual renewal, or even deliverance from God's wrath. Understanding exactly what we are being delivered from helps us appreciate the full impact of the gospel. To truly understand this promise, we must explore what the Bible says about deliverance and its profound implications.

THE WRATH OF GOD: UNDERSTANDING PAUL'S MESSAGE

In Rom 1:16, Paul begins by proclaiming the gospel as God's power for deliverance. In verse 17, he adds, "For in [it] the righteousness of God is revealed from faith to faith" (NASB). Here, Paul emphasizes that righteousness is revealed through faith. But in verse 18, Paul takes a sharp turn: "For the wrath of God is revealed from heaven against all ungodliness and unrighteousness of men who suppress the truth in unrighteousness" (NASB).

There's a natural flow here in Paul's message: first, he emphasizes righteousness through faith, and then he quickly turns to address God's wrath against unrighteousness. This isn't just about escaping God's wrath; it's about embracing his righteousness through faith, which leads to transformation. Paul seems to be contrasting two paths: those who live by faith and experience God's righteousness and those who reject it, experiencing the consequences of unrighteousness. This raises an important question: is Paul's message primarily about avoiding divine anger or inviting us into a deeper, transformative deliverance that changes how we live?

HISTORICAL INFLUENCES ON THE CONCEPT OF WRATH

We need to dig deeper into the term to understand what Paul means by wrath. In Rom 1:18, the Greek word for wrath is *orge*, which isn't just a burst of anger but reflects a person's character or nature. *Orge* refers to something deeper—God's holy character, revealed in response to unrighteousness. This helps us see that Paul isn't merely talking about anger; he's talking about how God's holiness contrasts with human sin.

But how did we end up seeing God's wrath as sheer anger or retribution? Much of it concerns how the Bible was translated and the historical influences that shaped those translations. In 1604, King James I of England commissioned scholars to translate the Bible into English. Earlier translations like the Geneva Bible influenced their work, and many of these translators viewed God through the lens of an angry, vengeful judge.

This perception of God as a wrathful figure has deep roots. When Constantine legalized Christianity in the fourth century, many of the emperor's attributes—his harsh enforcement of laws and retributive justice—were projected onto God. The church began to equate breaking Roman law with incurring wrath, which was applied to God's law. Influenced by these ideas, the translators of the King James Bible naturally translated *orge* as wrath, interpreting God as a figure of anger. This shaped how people understood God's nature and influenced Christian doctrine.

This view of God as a wrathful judge, mirroring the legalistic, retributive justice of Rome, trickled down through translations like the King James Bible. For example, J. I. Packer in *Knowing God* describes God's wrath as "retributive action" against those who defy him. However, this interpretation misses the fact that *orge* is a noun describing God's character, not a verb implying vengeful action. By misunderstanding this, many have distorted God into a figure of punishment rather than a holy and just God.

GOD'S CHARACTER REVEALED THROUGH JESUS

Given these misunderstandings of God's wrath, it's important to look at what the Bible actually says about God's character, particularly through Jesus. Hebrews 1:1-3 tells us that Jesus is *"the radiance of God's glory and the exact representation of his being."* This means that Jesus shows us exactly who God is.

So, what does Jesus reveal about God's character? John 3:16-17 tells us: *"For God so loved the world, that he gave his only Son, that whoever believes in him shall not perish but have eternal life. For God did not send his Son into the world to condemn the world, but to save the world through him."* This passage clearly shows that God's nature is rooted in love and salvation, not condemnation. The heart of the gospel is about abundant life (John 10:10), not judgment.

Jesus came as the ultimate expression of God's love—not to appease God's anger but to demonstrate his grace and mercy. First John 4:10 clarifies this: "In this is love, not that we loved God, but that he loved us and sent his Son to be the propitiation for our sins" (NASB). The word *propitiation* here doesn't mean appeasing anger but refers to God's active grace. The original Greek word *hilasmos* means "mercy" or "active grace," not a payoff for sin.

THE MEANING OF PROPITIATION: ACTIVE GRACE, NOT APPEASEMENT

The idea that Jesus died to appease God's wrath comes from misunderstandings of the word *propitiation*. The real meaning of *hilasmos* is about God's proactive grace in dealing with our sins, not about satisfying divine anger. Jesus didn't die to pay off God's wrath; he died to reunite us with God, restoring our relationship and making us heirs to his kingdom.

GOD'S PLAN OF RECONCILIATION THROUGH CHRIST

Second Corinthians 5:17–21 paints a beautiful picture of reconciliation: *"Therefore, if anyone is in Christ, he is a new creature; the old things passed away; behold, new things have come. Now all these things are from God, who reconciled us to himself through Christ"* (NASB). The Greek word for "reconcile" here means to make an exchange. In Christ, our sins are exchanged for his righteousness so that we become new creations in God's kingdom.

Ephesians 2:1–6 further emphasizes that God was already at work even when we were still in sin, reconciling us to himself. This reveals God's true character—not as an angry judge, but as a loving reconciler. God's ultimate goal is to restore us to himself, not to punish us.

THE JUDGMENT OF UNBELIEF

Does this mean no consequences exist for those who reject God's grace? John 3:17–21 makes it clear: *"He who does not believe has been judged already"* (NASB). This judgment reflects the free will

God gives us. Jesus didn't come to judge the world but to save it. However, the choice is still ours—to believe in him or reject him.

But what does it mean that those who don't believe are "judged already?" It means judgment isn't something that only happens in the future—it's already happening now. When someone chooses not to believe in Jesus, they remain separated from the life and purpose God has for them. This separation is the judgment itself, not some punishment God actively hands down. The judgment is simply the natural consequence of rejecting the offer of salvation and continuing to live outside God's design.

John 3:19 explains this further: "This is the judgment, that the Light has come into the world, and men loved the darkness rather than the Light" (NASB). God's judgment isn't about condemning people—it's about allowing them to remain in the darkness they've chosen by rejecting Jesus, the Light. They are already judged because they've chosen to reject the truth and stay separated from God's grace, preferring the darkness over the Light.

ROMANS 1:18 AND GOD'S WRATH AS SEPARATION

Romans 1:18 tells us that *"the wrath of God is revealed from heaven against all the godlessness and wickedness of people."* As discussed earlier, this wrath isn't about God lashing out in anger or punishing people. It's a reflection of the contrast between those who live in alignment with God's design and those who choose to reject his truth. The Greek word *orge*, translated as "wrath," refers to how God's holy character naturally responds to human unrighteousness—not as an outburst of anger but as the result of living outside of his purpose.

When Paul talks about God's wrath being revealed, he's showing us that God's holiness is revealed through those who live by faith. In Rom 1:17, Paul explains that God's righteousness is revealed *"from faith to faith,"* meaning his holiness becomes visible through the lives of people who live by faith, following his design and purpose. This isn't just about believing—it's about living in a way that reflects who God is and how he designed us to live.

God's holiness shines through those who live by faith. For those who accept that light, it brings life and clarity. But for those who reject it, that same light exposes how far they've chosen to live from God's purpose. It's not that God is angrily punishing them—it's that his holiness reveals the separation that comes from living outside of his design.

We've already discussed how rejecting God's truth has natural consequences. When we choose to live outside of his design, we experience separation, brokenness, and the absence of the life God offers. This is what Paul describes as wrath. It's not about God actively punishing people—it's the outcome of living apart from his design. God's holiness, revealed through those who live by faith, naturally exposes the consequences of unrighteousness, making clear the difference between truth and rejection.

When we talk about God's wrath, we're really talking about the natural result of his holiness being revealed. It's not about anger or rage—it's about how God's perfect design for life stands in contrast to the brokenness of living outside of it. Those who reject God's truth are choosing to live outside of his purpose, and the result of that choice is the separation they experience from his life and goodness.

THE CONSEQUENCES OF REJECTING GOD'S GRACE

When people choose to reject God's grace, Rom 1:24 explains that "God [gives] them over" to their own desires. This doesn't mean God is actively punishing them. Instead, it's like the rescue team that had to leave John Jones in the cave after every attempt to save him failed and he died: God lets people follow the path they've chosen. He doesn't force us to choose his way; he respects our free will.

When someone rejects God's grace, they continue on their own path, just like those in Rom 1 who exchanged the truth of

God for a lie. This isn't about divine punishment but rather the natural consequence of rejecting God's design. God allows them to follow the course they've chosen, respecting their free will even though that choice leads away from his life-giving purpose.

Verses 18–32 explain the full picture of what happens when people continue rejecting God. They gradually turn further from his purpose, and as a result, their lives reflect the distortion of truth and separation from his design. This is the end result of choosing to live apart from God's truth—not a display of divine wrath, but a revelation of the brokenness that comes when we live outside of his intended plan.

CONCLUSION

In this chapter, we've explored Paul's message in Rom 1 about God's character and how his holiness is revealed. The gospel is about deliverance and transformation, not just escaping wrath. The wrath of God (*orge*) is a reflection of his holy character, contrasting with human unrighteousness, not a vengeful response.

We've also seen that historical misunderstandings have skewed our view of God's nature, turning him into a figure of retribution. But Scripture, especially through Jesus, reveals God's true nature—full of love, grace, and a desire to reconcile us to himself. The judgment we face is not about God's anger but the result of our own choices to either accept or reject his gift of salvation.

Ultimately, God's plan is one of restoration, not condemnation. Through faith, we are invited to live according to his original design and experience the fullness of life he offers.

CHAPTER 2 STUDY QUESTIONS

1. **Understanding Salvation as Deliverance:** Paul describes the gospel as "the power of God for salvation," which also means deliverance. What do you think we are delivered from

through the gospel? How does this understanding impact your view of what it means to be saved?

2. **The Wrath of God:** This chapter explores how God's "wrath" is often misunderstood. Rather than retributive anger, it reflects God's holy character in response to sin. How does this perspective of God's wrath change or clarify your view of his character?

3. **Historical Perceptions of God's Wrath:** The chapter mentions how historical influences, like Roman legalism and translations like the King James Bible, shaped perceptions of God as an angry judge. How might these views impact our relationship with God today? Have you experienced or seen these ideas influence how people view God?

4. **Jesus as the Representation of God's Character:** Jesus shows us the true nature of God, emphasizing love, mercy, and grace. Reflecting on John 3:16–17 and 1 John 4:10, how does Jesus's life and message shape your understanding of who God is? How does this differ from traditional views of God's wrath?

5. **Propitiation and Active Grace:** The word *propitiation* is reinterpreted in this chapter as God's "active grace" rather than appeasement. How does understanding Jesus's sacrifice as an act of grace rather than a means of pacifying God affect your view of his purpose and role in salvation?

6. **The Consequences of Rejecting Grace:** The chapter discusses judgment as a natural consequence of choosing to live outside God's design. How does this view of judgment, as self-chosen separation rather than punishment, impact your understanding of free will and the choices we make?

7. **Living in Alignment with God's Design:** Paul's message in Romans highlights the importance of living according to God's design. What are some areas in your life where you sense a need to realign with God's purpose? How does the gospel empower you to make that realignment?

8. **Transformation over Escape:** This chapter emphasizes that the gospel's power is about transformation, not just escaping wrath. How does this understanding of salvation impact the way you view faith, repentance, and your relationship with God?

9. **God's Respect for Free Will:** The chapter concludes with a discussion on God allowing us to pursue our chosen paths, even if they lead away from him. How does this concept of God respecting free will resonate with you? How might it influence the way you approach your own decisions?

CHAPTER 3

The Kingdom of God

UNDERSTANDING THE KINGDOM OF GOD

To FULLY GRASP WHAT it means to live as citizens of the Kingdom of God, we first need to understand how the Bible defines this kingdom. The Kingdom of God is God's sovereign rule over all creation, which broke into the world through the life and ministry of Jesus. This kingdom isn't a physical realm but a spiritual reign where God's values and purposes are realized in the lives of his people. It's not like earthly kingdoms that rise and fall with time. Instead, it's eternal, transforming lives and shaping how we live today.

You'll notice that both the phrases "Kingdom of God" and "kingdom of heaven" are used throughout the New Testament. Understanding the context behind these terms helps us get a fuller picture of God's reign.

HEAVENLY AND EARTHLY KINGDOMS

The Gospel of Matthew frequently uses the phrase "kingdom of heaven." For example, in Matt 4:17, Jesus begins his ministry by saying, "Repent, for the kingdom of heaven has come near." Later, he says, "Blessed are the poor in spirit, for theirs is the kingdom of heaven" (Matt 5:3) and compares the kingdom to a hidden treasure of great value (Matt 13:44). Matthew's choice of the phrase "kingdom of heaven" reflects the Jewish audience he was writing for. In Jewish tradition, out of reverence for God's name, they often used the word "heaven" instead of directly saying "God." But make no mistake, "kingdom of heaven" and "Kingdom of God" point to the same thing—God's sovereign rule over all.

Mark and Luke, writing for broader audiences, use the "Kingdom of God" to make it clear that this reign wasn't just a future hope for a distant time—it was happening in their midst. In Mark 1:15, Jesus declares, "The time is fulfilled, and the Kingdom of God is at hand; repent and believe in the gospel" (NASB). This wasn't just something to wait for; it was already breaking into human history through Jesus.

Luke, too, emphasizes the present reality of the kingdom. In Luke 17:20–21, Jesus says, "The Kingdom of God is not coming with signs to be observed . . . for behold, the Kingdom of God is in your midst" (NASB). Jesus was clear: God's kingdom wasn't just a far-off promise but something unfolding right before their eyes. It was a kingdom that broke down cultural and religious barriers, inviting everyone to experience God's reign.

THE SPIRITUAL NATURE OF THE KINGDOM OF GOD

Paul, in his letters, brings a deeper understanding of the spiritual nature of God's kingdom. In Rom 14:17, he writes, "For the Kingdom of God is not eating and drinking, but righteousness and peace and joy in the Holy Spirit" (NASB). Paul is shifting the focus away from outward practices and traditions to the internal transformation that happens when we live in alignment with God's purposes. The Kingdom of God, according to Paul, is about a changed heart, transformed by God's Spirit. It's about living out God's values of righteousness, peace, and joy—qualities that come from deep within.

Together, these Scriptures show us that God's kingdom is not just a future hope but a present reality that began unfolding through Jesus and continues to shape our lives today. It is about living in the light of God's rule here and now, even as we wait for its full realization in the future.

PROPHETIC GLIMPSES OF THE KINGDOM IN THE OLD TESTAMENT

While we often think of the Kingdom of God as something introduced in the New Testament, its roots stretch deep into the Old Testament. The Bible gives us glimpses of this kingdom long before Jesus arrived. In Gen 14, Abraham encounters Melchizedek, a mysterious king and priest, and offers him a tithe from his battle spoils. Later, Ps 110 elevates Melchizedek to almost divine status, and Heb 5:6 compares him to Christ. This connection shows us that God's kingdom has always been a part of his plan.

Throughout the Psalms, particularly in Ps 2, we see descriptions of a king whose reign goes far beyond any earthly ruler. This points to a future king whose dominion would stretch over all creation—a prophecy ultimately fulfilled in Christ, as described in Heb 1. From the beginning, God's kingdom has been about more than earthly power; it's about his eternal rule that surpasses all human realms.

THE ETERNAL KINGDOM: GOD'S REIGN THROUGH CHRIST

Jesus often spoke about the Kingdom of God, making it clear that it wasn't just a future reality but something relevant right now. The Kingdom of God exists wherever Jesus is present—whether through his Spirit in the church or anywhere in the world. While the church plays an essential role in advancing the kingdom, it is not confined to the church. God's reign extends far beyond our church walls, touching every corner of creation. It's a kingdom that is both present and yet to come.

BELIEVERS AS AMBASSADORS OF THE KINGDOM

As believers, we are called to be ambassadors of this kingdom. The church often serves as the first point of contact where people encounter God's kingdom, but the kingdom isn't limited to church activities. We represent God's reign in everything we do—in our workplaces, communities, and families. Ephesians 1:23 reminds us that the church is Christ's body, created for good works (Eph 2:10) that reflect his rule. Our mission is more than outreach; we are called to reveal "the manifold wisdom of God . . . through the church to the rulers and authorities in the heavenly places" (Eph 3:10, NASB).

THE FUTURE PHYSICAL KINGDOM

To fully understand the Kingdom of God, we need to look back to Dan 2. In this passage, King Nebuchadnezzar had a dream about a giant statue representing various earthly kingdoms. Daniel interpreted this dream and explained that all these kingdoms would one day be destroyed by a kingdom that would never end—God's eternal kingdom. Daniel says, "In the days of those kings, the God of heaven will set up a kingdom which will never be destroyed . . . it will crush and put an end to all these kingdoms, but it will itself endure forever" (Dan 2:44, NASB).

This prophecy aligns with Jesus's proclamation of the Kingdom of God—a kingdom that surpasses all earthly powers and will last forever. Revelation 11:15 affirms this truth when it declares, *"The kingdom of the world has become the kingdom of our Lord and his Messiah, and he will reign for ever and ever."*

While the Kingdom of God is already at work, Rev 11:15 also points to its future fulfillment when God's reign will be fully established, and all things will be restored. We live in the tension between this present kingdom and the kingdom that is yet to come.

THE PRESENT YET FUTURE REALITY OF THE KINGDOM

Understanding that the Kingdom of God is already here but not fully realized changes how we live today. It shifts our focus from short-term, earthly goals to living with God's eternal purpose in mind. We are part of a kingdom that exists now, and this truth calls us to live lives that reflect God's reign in everything we do right here and right now.

Every day, our actions, decisions, and relationships should be shaped by the values of God's kingdom—righteousness, peace, and joy in the Holy Spirit. Our goal is not to simply wait for the kingdom to arrive in the future but to live in a way that shows the world its reality today.

At the same time, knowing that the kingdom will one day be fully established gives us hope. We still face difficulties and live in a broken world, but we trust that God's reign will be fully realized and will restore everything. This hope strengthens us to endure challenges with confidence, knowing God's promises are true.

We live in this tension of the "already but not yet"—God's kingdom is here, but it hasn't been fully revealed. This balance calls us to live with purpose now, advancing God's reign while holding on to the hope of its future fulfillment.

As we've seen, the Kingdom of God isn't something we're just waiting for—it's already here, changing the world through Jesus's victory over sin and death. Through his life, death, and resurrection, Jesus brought God's reign to earth, and he invites us to be part of it. But being part of the kingdom is more than just believing in it—it means living under God's rule and reflecting his values in our lives.

This understanding of the kingdom leads to something even deeper: personal transformation. When we enter God's kingdom, it changes not just how we see the world but who we are. Our identity is transformed, and we are called to live out this kingdom reality in our everyday lives. We are no longer just believers—we are people whose very identity has been redefined by God's rule.

CONCLUSION

The Kingdom of God is not just a future hope; it's a present reality that redefines how we live. It transforms our identity, reshapes our priorities, and guides our daily lives. We are not meant to be passive, waiting for the kingdom to come—we are ambassadors, advancing God's reign through our actions and purpose.

This kingdom changes us from the inside out. Whether we call it the "Kingdom of God" or the "kingdom of heaven," the message is the same: God's reign is here, breaking into our lives and calling us to live differently. It's not just a theological idea; it's a way of life that reflects God's priorities of righteousness, peace, and joy.

We've seen that God's kingdom has deep roots, stretching back to the Old Testament and fulfilled in the teachings of Jesus and Paul. Now, as believers, we are part of that eternal kingdom, chosen to reflect his rule in everything we do. Our actions matter—they show the world what living under God's reign looks like.

While we live in this present kingdom, we also hold on to the hope that one day God's reign will be fully realized. This "already but not yet" reality gives us the confidence to face challenges, knowing that God's kingdom will be complete. As we wait, we continue to live as citizens of his kingdom, actively advancing his reign on earth.

In the end, the Kingdom of God changes everything about how we live. It redefines our identity, our purpose, and our outlook on life. As God's workmanship, created for good works, we play a role in revealing his kingdom to the world. Our mission isn't just to talk about the kingdom—it's to live it out, showing the world the power of God's reign in every aspect of our lives.

The Kingdom of God

CHAPTER 3 STUDY QUESTIONS

1. **Defining the Kingdom:** The chapter describes the Kingdom of God as God's sovereign rule over creation. How does this understanding of the kingdom, as both present and spiritual, impact your view of God's role in the world today? What does it mean for you personally to live under God's rule?

2. **Heavenly vs. Earthly Kingdoms:** Jesus and the apostles spoke of the kingdom as a current reality. How does the "already but not yet" nature of the kingdom affect the way you live and make decisions in the present?

3. **Living as Kingdom Ambassadors:** As believers, we're called to be ambassadors of God's kingdom. What are some practical ways you can represent God's kingdom in your daily interactions and decisions—at work, in your community, and within your family?

4. **Old Testament Foundations:** This chapter highlights glimpses of God's kingdom in the Old Testament. How does seeing God's kingdom foreshadowed in stories like that of Melchizedek or in the Psalms deepen your understanding of its purpose and significance?

5. **The Kingdom's Spiritual Nature:** Paul emphasizes that the kingdom is not about external practices but internal transformation. How does living in righteousness, peace, and joy reflect God's kingdom in you? Are there specific areas in your life where you feel called to grow in these qualities?

6. **Transformation of Identity:** The Kingdom of God not only changes how we see the world but also redefines who we are. How has your identity as a citizen of God's kingdom influenced your sense of purpose, values, or priorities?

7. **Balancing the Present and Future Kingdom:** We live with the hope of a future, fully realized kingdom. How does this hope encourage you during difficult times? How can it shape the way you view challenges or setbacks in your life?

8. **Reflecting Kingdom Values:** The chapter discusses values like righteousness, peace, and joy as core to kingdom living. In what ways can you actively incorporate these values in your everyday actions and relationships?

9. **The Role of the Church:** This chapter suggests that while the kingdom extends beyond the church, the church plays a central role in advancing it. How do you see the church contributing to God's kingdom? How can you personally participate in this mission?

10. **Living the Kingdom Now:** What specific actions or changes might help you live out the reality of God's kingdom today? How can you actively demonstrate God's reign in your words, behavior, or mindset?

CHAPTER 4

Kingdom Citizens

ONCE WE ENTER GOD'S kingdom, everything about us changes. Our identity, our purpose, and our mission are all transformed. Being part of the kingdom means more than simply having a title—it's about living out who we truly are in Christ. Understanding the bigger picture of God's kingdom naturally leads us to see how it reshapes us from the inside out. We aren't the same as we once were.

In this chapter, we'll examine how being a citizen of God's kingdom completely changes our identity. We're not just bystanders; we're God's own children, heirs with a purpose and a calling that aligns with his eternal plan. This transformation impacts every part of our lives and calls us to live with the responsibility and mission that comes with being part of his kingdom.

The significance of God's kingdom is most evident in the way it transforms us as believers. It reshapes our behavior, identity, and sense of purpose, aligning us with God's divine design for our lives. This transformation is more than adopting a set of new habits—it's about becoming someone entirely new in the Kingdom of God. We move from being driven by the ways of this world to living out our true inheritance as *children of the King.*

Understanding this transformation is key because it sets the tone for everything else in our lives. Being part of God's kingdom isn't just something we study or talk about—it's something that redefines us. As kingdom citizens, we are called to reflect God's rule in everything we do, from our choices to our relationships and sense of mission in this world.

A NEW IDENTITY IN CHRIST: FROM SLAVES TO HEIRS

When we talk about transformation, it's not enough to think of it as merely changing our outward actions. The Bible teaches that our entire identity has been made new in Christ. We've been adopted into God's family and given a purpose in his kingdom. To fully grasp the depth of this change, we need to understand what Scripture says about who we are now that we belong to Christ.

Take 2 Cor 5:17: "If anyone is in Christ, he is a new creation; the old has gone, the new has come!" (NASB). This passage shows us that this transformation isn't just a surface change—it's a total rebirth. We are no longer defined by our past or the world's standards but by who we are in Christ. The *old self* is gone, and something entirely new has come into being.

Paul emphasizes this in Eph 2:10, where he reminds us that we are "God's workmanship," created for good works that God has prepared for us. The word "workmanship" in the Greek *poiēma* means a *masterpiece* or *work of art*, showing how intricately God has designed our lives. Just like skilled artists carefully craft each detail of their creation, God has created us with purpose and intention.

This idea ties in closely with the Greek word *ergon*, meaning "work" or "task." As we consider our place in God's kingdom, we see that we were designed to *fit perfectly* into his plan. Just like *ergonomics*—the study of designing something to fit its user perfectly—God has woven our gifts, talents, and lives into his kingdom work. We are his *ergon*, his masterpiece, designed for good works that align with his plan. And these good works aren't just something we do—they flow from the very core of who we are now in Christ.

JESUS AS OUR KINSMAN-REDEEMER

A key biblical concept that beautifully illustrates this transformation is that of the *kinsman-redeemer*. In the Old Testament, the kinsman-redeemer had the role of rescuing a family member from slavery or redeeming lost property to restore their place in the family. The story of *Boaz and Ruth* is one of the most well-known examples. Boaz steps in as Ruth's kinsman-redeemer, restoring her and ensuring that her family's legacy is protected.

In the same way, *Jesus is our ultimate kinsman-redeemer*. He didn't just rescue us from the slavery of sin—he restored our inheritance as *sons and daughters of God*. His death and resurrection secured not just our freedom but our place in *God's family*, giving us a share in his eternal kingdom.

The idea of the kinsman-redeemer is echoed in Gal 4:4–7, which tells us that through Jesus, we've been adopted into God's family: "But when the fullness of time had come, God sent forth his Son, born of a woman, born under the law, to redeem those under the law, so that we might receive adoption as sons. And because you are sons, God has sent the Spirit of his Son into our hearts, crying, 'Abba! Father!' So you are no longer a slave, but a son, and if a son, then an heir through God" (NASB).

What's striking here is that we are not just redeemed from sin—we are brought into the very family of God. We are made *heirs*. Just as Boaz restored Ruth's family line and secured their future, *Jesus secured our place in God's eternal kingdom*. Through him, we have been given the *inheritance of righteousness* and the rights of children adopted into the *family of God*.

SEATED WITH CHRIST: A NEW POSITION OF AUTHORITY

Not only has Jesus redeemed us, but he has also given us a completely new spiritual position. Ephesians 2:6 tells us that we've been "raised up and seated with Christ in the heavenly realms." This isn't just a nice spiritual metaphor—it's a powerful statement of who we are now. Being seated with Christ means we share in his authority. The limitations of this world no longer bind us—we live under the rule and reign of Jesus. Our position with him empowers us to live out the kingdom's values right now.

This new position also reflects our adoption into God's family. Ephesians 1:5 makes it clear that through Jesus, we've been *adopted as sons and daughters*. Our identity is no longer shaped by the world but by our relationship with the Father. We are heirs of everything he has promised, and we share in the inheritance of the kingdom.

Paul also reminds us in Eph 1:13 that we've been *sealed with the Holy Spirit*. This seal is God's mark of ownership over us and a guarantee of our inheritance. It's a constant reminder that we belong to him and that our future is secure. Through the Holy Spirit, we are given the power to live out our new identity as *kingdom citizens*, reflecting God's reign in our lives.

UNITY AND SERVICE IN THE KINGDOM

This transformation extends beyond us individually—it's meant to shape the entire Body of Christ. As Paul explains in Eph 4:1–16, we are called to live out this new identity in unity with other believers, serving one another as we grow spiritually. Each of us has a role to play in God's kingdom. Living in unity reflects God's kingdom values—humility, patience, gentleness, and love. Unity isn't just a nice idea—it's at the heart of what it means to be kingdom citizens.

Paul shows us that our unity isn't just for the sake of community—it equips us for service. Jesus gave us different roles within the church—not so that we could focus on titles but to build up the Body of Christ. Every one of us has a part to play, and as we live out our calling, we help one another grow in faith and maturity.

Many examples in the New Testament show us what this looks like in practice. For instance, in the parable of the good Samaritan (Luke 10:25–37), Jesus tells the story of a man who is beaten and left for dead on the side of the road. While others pass him by, it's the Samaritan—someone considered an outsider—who stops to help. He cares for the man, not out of obligation, but out of genuine compassion and love. This parable is a powerful picture of what it means to love our neighbor, demonstrating that as citizens of God's kingdom, we are called to show kindness and mercy to those in need, regardless of their background.

Another example comes from Jesus's own life when he washed the feet of his disciples (John 13:1–17). This act of service was unexpected, especially coming from the one they called Lord and Teacher. Yet, Jesus knelt down and took on the role of a servant, teaching his disciples that true greatness in the kingdom comes from serving others. As citizens of God's kingdom, we follow this example by humbling ourselves and putting the needs of others before our own, just as Jesus did.

We also see this lived out in the early church (Acts 2:42–47). The believers were deeply committed to one another, sharing their possessions and resources so that no one was in need. They gathered together, broke bread, and devoted themselves to prayer and the apostles' teaching. Their unity and generosity were clear expressions of what it means to live in God's kingdom. They didn't just talk about love and service—they embodied it in how they lived and cared for each other.

These examples illustrate that being a citizen of God's kingdom isn't just about a title or a set of beliefs—it's about living in a way that reflects God's values of love, service, and unity. Whether we're showing compassion to a neighbor, serving humbly, or living in community with other believers, we are called to live out the kingdom in tangible, practical ways.

MATURING AS CITIZENS OF THE KINGDOM

As citizens of God's kingdom, we're called to grow in spiritual maturity. Ephesians 4:15–16 urges us to grow up in every way into Christ, who is the head of the body. Paul warns against staying spiritually immature, swayed by every new teaching or deceitful scheme. Instead, we're called to stand firm, speak the truth in love, and grow into the fullness of Christ.

This growth is essential because it equips us to reflect Christ more fully in everything we do. The more we grow, the more we align with God's purpose and design for our lives. As we mature, we become stronger and more capable of standing firm in our faith and living out the good works that God prepared for us.

As we've explored, being citizens of God's kingdom transforms everything about who we are. Our new identity in Christ, our unity with other believers, and our call to live out the values of the kingdom shape every part of our lives. But this transformation isn't a one-time event—it's a journey of growth. Just as we are called to live out God's rule in our actions and relationships, we are also called to mature in our faith. This process of spiritual maturity equips us to reflect God's kingdom more fully and prepares us for the deeper work of advancing his purposes in the world.

CONCLUSION

In the Kingdom of God, we are not just passive recipients of his grace. We are active participants, called to live in a way that reflects his reign. Jesus, our kinsman-redeemer, has redeemed us from sin, restored our inheritance, and given us the Holy Spirit to empower us as his children. Our identity is no longer shaped by this world but by our relationship with our Father in heaven.

As we grow in spiritual maturity, we begin to reflect more of Christ's character. This growth isn't just for our personal benefit—it's meant to bring God's healing and restoration to the world around us. Spiritual maturity prepares us to live out our calling with wisdom and strength, equipping us to be agents of his kingdom in every situation.

The journey doesn't end with transformation. It continues as we grow in Christ, learning to walk in the fullness of his kingdom and advance his reign on earth. In the next chapter, we will explore how this growth—this deepening of our spiritual maturity—prepares us to bring the Kingdom of God into the world in even more impactful ways. Living as kingdom citizens is just the beginning;

growing into spiritual maturity is how we become effective in the work God has set before us.

CHAPTER 4 STUDY QUESTIONS

1. **New Identity in Christ:** The chapter describes our identity as transformed in Christ, moving from "slaves" to "heirs." What does this new identity mean to you personally, and how does it change the way you view yourself and your purpose?

2. **The Role of the Kinsman-Redeemer:** Jesus is described as our kinsman-redeemer, securing our place in God's family. How does understanding Jesus in this role deepen your appreciation for what he has done? In what ways can this understanding impact your daily walk with him?

3. **Seated with Christ:** Ephesians 2:6 tells us we are "seated with Christ." What do you think this position of authority means for your life? How does it empower you to live out kingdom values and make decisions aligned with God's purpose?

4. **Unity and Service in the Kingdom:** Unity and service are central to life in the kingdom. How can you actively contribute to unity within your church or faith community? Are there specific acts of service you feel called to pursue?

5. **Living Kingdom Values:** The chapter highlights the values of God's kingdom, such as love, compassion, humility, and service. How can you reflect these values in practical ways this week? Is there someone in your life who might need to experience one of these qualities?

6. **Maturing as Kingdom Citizens:** Spiritual maturity is described as essential to living out our kingdom identity. What steps can you take to grow in spiritual maturity? Are there areas of your faith where you feel particularly called to deepen your understanding or commitment?

7. **Learning from Biblical Examples:** Reflecting on the examples of the good Samaritan, Jesus washing his disciples' feet,

and the early church, how do these examples challenge or inspire you to live out kingdom principles? Are there specific lessons you can apply to your life?

8. **Reflecting God's Kingdom in Daily Life:** As citizens of God's kingdom, we're called to live out our new identity in every part of our lives. What are some ways you can demonstrate your identity as a kingdom citizen in your relationships, work, or community?

9. **Growing in Christlikeness:** The chapter mentions that maturing in faith equips us to reflect Christ's character more fully. What aspects of Christ's character do you find most challenging to embody? How can you work on integrating these traits into your life?

10. **Purpose in God's Kingdom:** How does knowing that you're "God's workmanship, created for good works" affect your sense of mission and purpose? Are there specific gifts or talents you feel God is calling you to use for his kingdom?

CHAPTER 5

Citizens with a Purpose

THE LAST CHAPTER EXPLORED how being part of God's kingdom transforms our identity. When we place our faith in Christ, we are completely changed. We are made new: "The old has gone, the new is here" (2 Cor 5:17). Our position shifts as we become new creations in Christ. As Paul says in Col 2:9–10, "In him all the fullness of God lives in bodily form, and in him, you have been made complete" (NASB). This reminds us that we are whole in Christ, fully equipped to live the new life he has called us to. In this chapter, we'll focus on growing in spiritual maturity—understanding the blessings of being chosen and adopted by God, the redemption we have in Christ, and how God reveals his will to us. We'll also look at how the Holy Spirit actively works in our lives, empowering us to live out our purpose as citizens of his kingdom.

RENEWING THE MIND

Even though our identity transformation is complete, we still need to let go of the old ways of thinking. It's like detoxing from the world's patterns—retraining our minds to align with the reality of who we already are in Christ. This process, though challenging, is a source of encouragement and motivation. While our spiritual transformation is finished, the renewal of our minds helps us live out this new identity daily.

This process is crucial to our growth as believers. We aren't striving to become something new; we're learning to live in the truth of who we already are. As we renew our minds, we become more aware of our place in God's plan.

PAUL'S PRAYER FOR ENLIGHTENMENT

This is why Paul prayed for us that "the eyes of our hearts would be enlightened" so that we can truly grasp "the hope of his calling, the riches of the glory of his inheritance in the saints, and the surpassing greatness of his power toward us who believe" (Eph 1:18–19, NASB). Paul understood that this revelation is essential for us to fully live in the reality of who we are in Christ. It empowers us to walk confidently in God's power and purpose.

SPIRITUAL BLESSINGS IN CHRIST

Our understanding of this flows directly from the "spirit of wisdom and revelation," which comes from experiencing a more profound "knowledge of him" (Eph 1:17). This knowledge is connected to the spiritual blessings that God has already given us. In Eph 1, Paul opens our eyes to these blessings, offering a glimpse into what God has provided. These blessings reveal the truth of who we are as new creations in Christ. Knowing them helps us to align our beliefs with the reality of who we are.

CHOSEN AND ADOPTED IN LOVE

In Eph 1:4–5, Paul reveals two essential spiritual blessings that show God's actions toward believers—his choosing and predestining. He begins by connecting these blessings with the phrase "just as," emphasizing that they both flow from God's love and grace.

First, Paul explains that God "chose us in him before the foundation of the world." This choice isn't about selecting specific individuals in the distant past. Instead, it highlights God's decision that those who place their faith in Christ would be set apart for his purposes. From the very beginning—before creation—God's desire was always for us to be part of his family, not as an afterthought, but as part of his eternal design. The goal of this choice is clear: that we would be "holy and blameless before him." God's intention is for believers to be transformed into people who reflect his character, living lives that are set apart and pure. This transformation is not about achieving perfection in the present but about becoming more like Christ as we follow him.

Paul then introduces the next blessing, linking it with the phrase "in love." He explains that God, "in love," predestined us for adoption as his children through Jesus Christ. This predestination is not about handpicking some people while excluding others. Rather, it means that God predetermined that all who believe in Christ would be adopted into his family. Adoption, in this context, carries a profound meaning. In Paul's culture, adoption granted full legal rights and status as a true family member. So, when Paul says we are adopted, he emphasizes that we are brought into God's family with all the rights and privileges that come with being his children.

Paul reminds us that all of this was done "according to the kind intention of his will." God didn't act reluctantly or out of obligation. It was his joy, driven by kindness and grace, to adopt us. Everything—from choosing us to predestining our adoption—flows out of his loving nature and purposeful plan for those who place their faith in Christ.

Paul paints a beautiful picture of God's intentional plan in these verses. God's choice to set us apart and adopt us wasn't a random act; it was part of his eternal, love-driven design. Through Christ, we've been welcomed into God's family, set apart, and made holy. Understanding this truth is key to grasping our identity and purpose in God's kingdom. This is the core message of the gospel that both John the Baptist and Jesus preached—a message of God's active love and plan to restore us.

REDEMPTION THROUGH CHRIST'S BLOOD

Paul continues unpacking the next spiritual blessing: "In him we have redemption through his blood, the forgiveness of sins" (Eph 1:7). Redemption here is more than just paying a ransom or settling a debt—it's about being set free. In Christ, we have been liberated from the bondage of sin and death. This isn't just about a transaction; it speaks to our transformation. Through Jesus's sacrifice, we are no longer slaves to sin, but we are freed to live out the fullness of the life that God intends for us.

This redemption is tied directly to the forgiveness of our sins. Through Christ's blood, God's abundant grace removes every mistake and failure, casting them away as far as the east is from the west (Ps 103:12).

It's not simply a removal of guilt but a complete restoration—allowing us to walk freely in the life God has designed for us. In this way, redemption brings freedom and restoration, setting us on a path to live as his children, fully aligned with his purposes.

REVEALING THE MYSTERY OF GOD'S WILL

Another blessing Paul mentions is that God has revealed his will to us (Eph 1:9). He hasn't left us to stumble through life aimlessly, unsure of our purpose. Instead, he has made known to us the mystery of his will, giving us a glimpse into his greater plan. This means we're not just living daily—we're part of something much bigger than ourselves, and we can move forward with confidence, knowing we have a role in God's unfolding purpose.

GOD'S ADMINISTRATION: *OIKONOMIA*

This understanding of God's will connects to a much larger idea—God's careful oversight of his plan for creation. Just as a household is managed and organized to ensure everything runs smoothly, God directs his creation with purpose and perfect timing. Nothing in his plan is random or without direction; every detail works together according to his greater purpose.

In Greek, this concept is called *oikonomia*, translated as "administration" in the New American Standard Bible translation. It refers to the management or stewardship of a household. Just like the head of a household ensures everything is in order, God, as the head of his household, oversees his grand plan for creation. When Paul talks about God revealing his will to us, he is showing that we've been brought into God's household, given insight into his work, and invited to participate in a plan that was in motion long before we even existed.

The concept of *oikonomia* reminds us that we're not just bystanders. The word itself speaks to the idea of a household managed by the one whose name it bears, like the house of David. In this sense, God is the head of his own household, overseeing the grand plan for his creation. Just as the house of David operated under the authority of its head, we, as members of God's household, live under his stewardship and direction. We've been entrusted not only with the knowledge of his will but also with a role in his kingdom. Much like household members who each have specific responsibilities, we are called to actively participate in God's administration, contributing to his kingdom with the resources, abilities, and insight he has given us. Through this, we join in the fulfillment of his divine plan, living out our purpose under the authority and care of his household.

SEALED WITH THE HOLY SPIRIT

Finally, Paul says that we've been sealed with the Holy Spirit (Eph 1:13). The Holy Spirit is God's mark on us, a guarantee of our inheritance in Christ. The Spirit isn't just a promise for the future but is actively working in our lives now, guiding, empowering, and ensuring that we have everything we need to fulfill God's purpose.

EXPERIENCING THE POWER OF GOD

In Eph 1:19, Paul talks about "the surpassing greatness of his power toward us who believe" (NASB). Paul points out that the same power that raised Jesus from the dead is available to us in real time. This power is at work in us through the Holy Spirit. Paul continues this thought in verses 20–23, making it clear that the resurrection power—the greatest display of God's strength—flows directly to us as believers.

The Holy Spirit is the source of this power in our lives. He strengthens us to overcome challenges, resist temptation, and fulfill God's purposes. This isn't a one-time event—the Spirit continually shapes and transforms us, guiding us each day to become more like Christ.

When we talk about the greatness of God's power, we're referring to the Holy Spirit's constant presence and influence in our lives. The Spirit is at the heart of our spiritual growth, helping us align our lives with God's will and his purposes. Through him, we're empowered to live for God and to deepen our understanding of who he is and how he works through us. His active involvement in our lives allows us to live out our faith in a way that brings glory to God in everything we do.

LIVING BY THE SPIRIT'S POWER

Galatians 5:22–23 tells us that when we live by the power of the Holy Spirit, we will bear fruit: "The Fruit of the Spirit is love, joy, peace, forbearance, kindness, goodness, faithfulness, gentleness and self-control." These qualities show the work of the Spirit in our lives, and they are evidence of his presence. Through this, we learn not just to live by the Spirit but to walk in the Spirit (Gal 5:25).

Many of us have probably heard, either directly or indirectly, that although we are new creations in Christ, we still have a sinful nature that remains with us until we reach heaven. This idea suggests that we're constantly torn between two natures—one part of us being new in Christ and the other still sinful and resistant to God's will. But that's not what the Bible teaches us about our identity in Christ.

Scripture tells us a different truth. In 2 Cor 5:17, we read, "If anyone is in Christ, the new creation has come: The old has gone, the new is here!" (NASB). This verse shows us that when we put our faith in Christ, we are made completely new. The old sinful nature no longer defines who we are. We're not a blend of sin and redemption—we are fully new creations, and the old way of life is gone.

Think of it like a balloon. Once a balloon is made, it stays a balloon whether it's filled with air or not. When the balloon is filled with air, it can fulfill its purpose. But when the air is let out, it's still a balloon—it's just not functioning the way it's supposed to. In the same way, when we come to Christ, we are made new—a transformed creation, much like the balloon. When we are filled with the Holy Spirit, we are equipped to function according to God's purpose and bear fruit in our lives. But when we live according to the flesh, we don't stop being new creations—we're just not filled with the Spirit and aren't producing the fruit we were meant to bear.

This explains why, even though our identity is fully transformed, we still struggle at times. Romans 12:2 tells us that our minds need renewal. When Paul talks about "the flesh," he's not referring to a sinful nature we still carry but to the old ways of thinking that need to be retrained. The habits and thoughts that once led us astray now need to be reshaped to align with the truth of who we are in Christ.

Romans 6:6 reminds us that our old self was crucified with Christ so that "we should no longer be slaves to sin." Our old sinful nature was put to death with Christ, so we are no longer controlled by sin. The struggles we face come from old patterns of thinking and habits, not from a sinful nature within us. As new creations, we've been freed from sin's power, and it's now about aligning our minds and actions with the new life we've received.

This is why Gal 5:16–18 tells us to "walk by the Spirit, and you will not gratify the desires of the flesh." Walking by the Spirit is not about battling a sinful nature; it's about letting the Holy Spirit lead us, transforming our minds and helping us live in the truth of our new identity. With the Spirit guiding us, we can live free from the old ways and fully embrace the life God has for us.

CONCLUSION

As we wrap up this chapter, it's clear that spiritual maturity isn't about trying to become something we're not—it's about stepping into the reality of who we already are in Christ. God has chosen us, adopted us, and redeemed us. He's revealed his will for our lives, and through the work of the Holy Spirit, we are empowered to live out this new identity. With the Spirit leading us, we can let go of the old patterns of thinking and embrace the life God has for us—one that's full of freedom, purpose, and fruitfulness. In Christ, we are complete, and as we walk by the Spirit, we live out that truth each day.

But even as we grow in this understanding and experience the Spirit's work in us, there are obstacles that can hinder us from walking fully in the Spirit's power. In the next chapter, we'll take a look at these obstacles, where they come from, and how we can overcome them as we continue on the path of spiritual maturity.

CHAPTER 5 STUDY QUESTIONS

1. **Understanding Our New Identity:** Reflect on 2 Cor 5:17, which describes us as "new creations" in Christ. What does this new identity mean to you? How does it affect the way you view your purpose and potential in God's kingdom?

2. **Renewing the Mind:** This chapter emphasizes the need to renew our minds, letting go of old thought patterns. Are there specific ways of thinking or habits you need to release to align more with your identity in Christ? How can renewing your mind help you live out your faith more fully?

3. **Chosen and Adopted:** Ephesians 1:4–5 speaks of being chosen and adopted by God. How does understanding your adoption as God's child impact the way you see yourself and your relationship with him?

4. **Redemption and Freedom:** Paul describes redemption as liberation from the bondage of sin. What does this freedom mean to you personally? Are there areas in your life where you're still learning to walk in this freedom?

5. **Revealing the Mystery of God's Will:** Ephesians 1:9–10 mentions that God has made known to us the mystery of his will. How does knowing that you are part of God's plan change your perspective on life? In what ways can you seek a clearer understanding of his purpose for you?

6. **Participating in God's Plan:** The concept of *oikonomia* (administration) reminds us that we are active participants in God's household. How can you contribute to God's kingdom with the resources, abilities, and opportunities he has given you?

7. **Sealed with the Holy Spirit:** Ephesians 1:13 describes the Holy Spirit as a seal and guarantee of our inheritance. How does the presence of the Holy Spirit assure you of your identity and guide you in living out God's purpose?

8. **Living by the Spirit's Power:** Galatians 5:22–23 describes the Fruit of the Spirit as evidence of his work in us. Are there specific qualities, such as love, joy, or self-control, that you feel called to cultivate? How can you actively walk in the Spirit to bear these fruits?

9. **The Role of Spiritual Maturity:** This chapter emphasizes that spiritual maturity is about stepping into the reality of who we

already are in Christ. What steps can you take to grow in this maturity? Are there areas where you feel particularly called to deepen your faith?

10. **Walking in Freedom:** The chapter explains that struggles often stem from old ways of thinking, not a sinful nature. How can you remind yourself of your freedom in Christ when facing challenges? What practical ways can help you overcome old patterns and fully embrace your new life in Christ?

CHAPTER 6

Overcoming Obstacles to Spiritual Maturity

In this chapter, we'll examine the obstacles that can slow our spiritual growth. We'll explore where these challenges come from, how they interfere with our walk with God, and practical ways to overcome them. Living fully in the Spirit means being aware of what holds us back and intentionally stepping into the freedom already ours in Christ.

IDENTIFYING SPIRITUAL OBSTACLES

Paul captures this idea in Rom 12:1-2, where he says, "Therefore, I urge you, brothers and sisters, in view of God's mercy, to offer your bodies as a living sacrifice, holy and pleasing to God—this is your true and proper worship. Do not conform to the pattern of this world, but be transformed by the renewing of your mind. Then you will be able to test and approve what God's will is—his good, pleasing, and perfect will."

In Romans, Paul is addressing Christians, implying that while believers are saved, they are still susceptible to conforming to the world's patterns. To grasp Paul's message fully, we need to consider the broader context. Romans 12:1-2 marks a pivotal shift in Paul's letter, transitioning from theological teaching to practical application. Here, Paul emphasizes that a true understanding of the gospel naturally compels believers toward transformed living—salvation brings not only freedom from sin's penalty but also its power. This transformation is not a secondary aspect of faith; it is central to the gospel itself. The transition from Rom 11 to 12 underscores this unity, moving from what God has done for us (his redemptive actions) to what we are called to do in response (Christian obedience). Paul's appeal highlights that God's grace sustains this journey of obedience, intertwining theological truth with practical living in our daily walk.[1]

CULTURAL PRESSURES THEN AND NOW

In Paul's time, Christians faced a variety of cultural, religious, and moral practices that clashed with their faith, urging them to live in ways contrary to societal norms. For instance, polytheistic practices and idol worship were pervasive in the Greco-Roman world, and refusing to participate often led to social alienation or persecution.[2] Sexual freedom and relativism were widely accepted, yet Christians were called to purity, setting them apart from common practices.[3] Additionally, while Roman society valued rigid social hierarchies, pride, and the pursuit of wealth, Christians were taught to embrace humility, service, and equality. Prevailing attitudes toward revenge clashed with Christ's call for forgiveness, requiring a radical reorientation of behavior.[4]

These "patterns of the world" profoundly shaped daily life, identity, and survival in Greco-Roman society. By encouraging Christians to resist these norms, Paul was calling them to a transformed, Christ-centered perspective that defined and distinguished their lives.

---

1. Moo, *Epistle*, 407–8.
2. Johnson, *Among the gentiles*, 20.
3. Scheidel, "A Peculiar Institution?," 280–91.
4. Lampe, "Social Welfare," 1–28.

Similarly, today's Christians are called to recognize and resist the world's patterns that subtly conflict with a Christ-centered life. While Paul faced societal pressures around idol worship, sexual freedom, and rigid hierarchies, our challenges today are no less impactful. Materialism and consumer culture tempt us to find identity in what we own rather than who we are in Christ.[5] Similarly, moral relativism promotes the idea that truth is flexible, contrasting with our foundation in absolute truth. Society elevates individualism and self-promotion, often emphasizing personal achievement over the humility and community values central to our faith.

The fast-paced digital age also fosters a desire for instant gratification, often at the cost of patience and spiritual discipline. Social media and online interactions can replace deeper, real-life connections, weakening the sense of community we are called to cultivate.[6] Additionally, political divides can distract us from kingdom-centered values, while media and entertainment frequently promote lifestyles that clash with biblical teachings. Our culture's emphasis on career success and personal achievement can lead us to prioritize society's definitions of accomplishment, sidelining the pursuit of God's purpose in our lives.

These cultural patterns pose real challenges, requiring discernment and commitment as we seek to live faithfully in a world that often promotes values contrary to the gospel.

LIVING OUT OUR FAITH IN PRACTICE

Paul recognized that believers continually face influences that pull their focus from God and tempt them to conform to the world's values. Yet Paul emphasized that true victory comes through a renewed mind—a deliberate shift toward God-centered thinking.

---

5. Miller, *Consuming Religion*. For further insights, see Landers, "Review of *Consuming Religion*."

6. Hudders and Pandelaere, "Silver Lining," 411–37.

This isn't a superficial change; it reshapes core beliefs, aligning thoughts and actions with God's purpose.

By investing in this transformation, believers invite the Holy Spirit to work powerfully within, guiding them toward spiritual maturity. Through this renewed perspective, they develop resilience against worldly influences, learning to live in a way that reflects their identity in Christ and fosters genuine spiritual growth.

In Rom 12:1, Paul's "therefore" acts as a powerful hinge between the theological foundation he had laid in the previous chapters and the practical call to action that follows. Up to this point, Paul has carefully unpacked the gospel message, revealing that broken and sinful humanity is redeemed solely by God's grace through faith in Christ (Rom 5:1–2). He demonstrates that our relationship with God has undergone a fundamental shift—from condemnation under the law to a life empowered by the Spirit (Rom 8). This shift isn't based on our own efforts but solely on God's mercy, which culminates in his promises to redeem both Israel and the gentiles (Rom 9–11).

With the word "therefore," Paul links this profound theological foundation to a life of response, urging believers to "offer [their] bodies as a living sacrifice, holy and pleasing to God" (Rom 12:1). This isn't a set of rules or rituals; it's a response to God's grace, a life transformed by a renewed mind. Paul's point is that salvation fundamentally reshapes who we are—our identity, values, and actions—and calls us to live in a way that reflects God's character. This response flows naturally from the mercy and grace we've received, becoming the practical expression of the theological truths Paul has laid out.

Paul's invitation to a "renewed mind" in Rom 12:2 goes beyond surface change; it's a radical reorientation to live in the new reality of who we are in Christ. His "therefore" captures this call to transformation: because of all that God has done, we're invited to live fully in the freedom he's given us, to walk in alignment with his will, and to resist the pressures of a world that constantly pulls us in the opposite direction.

Paul's words in Col 3:1–2 remind us to keep our hearts and minds centered on the things of God: "Since, then, you have been raised with Christ, set your hearts on things above, where Christ is, seated at the right hand of God. Set your minds on things above, not on earthly things." This aligns perfectly with Jesus's teaching in Matt 6:25–33, where he addresses the distractions and anxieties that can pull our focus away from God. Jesus acknowledged the realities of life—concerns about food, clothing, and other needs—but emphasized a kingdom-first perspective, saying, "Seek first God's kingdom and his righteousness, and all these things will be given to you as well."

In Rom 14:17, Paul continues this theme, underscoring what really matters in the Kingdom of God: "For the kingdom of God is not a matter of eating and drinking, but of righteousness, peace and joy in the Holy Spirit." These Scriptures together call us to orient our lives around kingdom values, focusing not on temporary or material things but on the deeper realities of righteousness, peace, and joy that God provides through his Spirit.

PULLING DOWN STRONGHOLDS

As we've discussed, the strong influence of worldly values and habits can pull us away from the path of spiritual growth, creating a significant obstacle to maturity. But external distractions aren't the only challenge.

Paul's words in 2 Cor 10:3–5, though initially spoken in defense against his critics, carry a powerful reminder for all believers. While he addressed accusations against his own ministry, his message reveals principles for dealing with the obstacles that every Christian encounters. In this passage, Paul extends his earlier teaching from Rom 12:1–2 on transformation and resisting the patterns of this world.

When Paul talks about "waging war" not in the flesh, he's showing that our battles and challenges aren't fought with ordinary human strategies but with the spiritual strength God supplies. This resonates with his urging in Romans to renew our minds, to keep our focus on God's will rather than worldly pressures.

In describing spiritual "warfare," Paul emphasizes the need to pull down anything that challenges God's truth, from misleading ideas to "lofty things" that push against what we know of God. Just as in Romans, where we're called to be living sacrifices, here Paul encourages a life actively submitted to Christ, where we take each thought captive and bring it into alignment with our faith. It's a call to confront any resistance that comes up within us—whether from old habits or cultural influences—and allow the Holy Spirit to reshape our thinking in line with God's truth.

The image of "destroying fortresses" gives us a picture of breaking down mental strongholds that distort our understanding of God. Paul reminds us not to rely on earthly wisdom or prideful thinking that opposes God's wisdom but to develop a mindset rooted in obedience to Christ. By actively renewing our minds and taking each thought captive, we resist the world's pull, allowing God's truth to shape our lives. This practice doesn't just echo Rom 12 but also empowers us to dismantle anything that stands in the way of growing mature in Christ.[7]

PUT ON THE ARMOR OF GOD

Paul's words in Eph 6:10–18 offer practical insight into how we can actively resist the influences that pull us away from spiritual maturity. He urges us to "be strong in the Lord" and rely on God's strength instead of our own. Through the metaphor of the "Armor of God," Paul reminds us that the challenges we face are not just physical or external but are often spiritual in nature, coming from forces that work against God's purposes.

The armor represents essential truths and virtues that we must hold on to—truth, righteousness, peace, faith, salvation, and the Word of God. These are not just concepts but active defenses

---

7. Alford, *Alford's Greek Testament*.

that equip us to "stand firm" against anything the enemy throws our way. Each piece, from the belt of truth to the sword of the Spirit, is crucial for living out our faith and overcoming the obstacles to spiritual growth.

Paul closes with a call to stay alert in prayer, bringing all our needs before God, who empowers us to stand firm. This readiness is at the core of spiritual growth: it's not a passive stance but an active, Spirit-filled way of engaging with the challenges we face, knowing that God's strength enables us to endure and grow.

CONCLUSION

In this chapter, we have explored the essential steps toward spiritual maturity: resisting worldly values and renewing our minds in Christ. This transformation allows us to live according to God's design, equipping us to stand firm in faith and to reflect his kingdom in a world that often opposes his values. As Rom 12:2 urges us, we are not to conform to worldly patterns but to let our minds be transformed by God's truth. By doing so, we align more closely with our identity in Christ and gain clarity in discerning his will.

As members of God's kingdom and his beloved children, we carry not only the blessings but also the responsibilities of this inheritance. Our role is active; we are called to represent God's kingdom here on earth. Paul reminds us in Rom 8:17, "If we are children, then we are heirs—heirs of God and co-heirs with Christ." This means that our inheritance is not just a future hope but a present calling that shapes how we engage with others, face challenges, and live with purpose.

By embracing our identity as heirs, we take on the role of ambassadors for Christ. Through a life transformed by his Spirit, we reflect the values of his kingdom, sharing his love, joy, and peace with those around us. In a world often marked by self-interest and discord, our commitment to renewing our minds and resisting worldly influences sets us apart and makes our witness impactful.

CHAPTER 6 STUDY QUESTIONS

1. **Understanding Your Identity in Christ**: What does being a "new creation" mean to you personally, and how does this understanding impact the way you live? (Reflect on 2 Cor 5:17.) Think about the concept of being an heir in God's kingdom (Rom 8:17). How does viewing yourself as part of God's family influence your actions and mindset? Share a time (or think about a scenario) where remembering your identity in Christ helped you overcome a challenge.

2. **Resisting Worldly Influences and Renewing Your Mind**: In Rom 12:2, Paul calls believers not to conform to the patterns of this world but to be transformed by the renewing of their minds. What are some specific ways you feel God calling you to renew your thinking? What worldly values or influences do you notice are most challenging to resist? Discuss how renewing your mind can strengthen your impact as an ambassador for Christ.

3. **The Armor of God as Practical Protection**: Read Eph 6:10–18 and consider each piece of the Armor of God. Which piece feels most important in your life right now, and why? Describe a recent situation where you felt spiritually under attack. How might applying the "armor" change your response in future situations? Share insights and pray over needs for strength, truth, or faith this week.

4. **Representing God's Kingdom as Ambassadors**: Paul calls believers ambassadors of Christ. How can this role shape the way you interact with people around you? What is one practical way you could reflect kingdom values—like righteousness, peace, and joy—in your community or relationships this week? Discuss practical ways to live as representatives of God's kingdom, and how renewing your mind strengthens your witness.

5. **Applying Lessons from This Chapter**: Think of one specific change you could make this week to grow spiritually. Is there

a habit you want to start, a mindset you want to change, or an area where you seek growth? Who could support you on this journey for accountability or encouragement? Consider checking in on progress, praying over growth and challenges.

CHAPTER 7

Renewing the Mind

A LIFE OF DEVOTION AND TRANSFORMATION

As we step into the journey of *renewing the mind*, Paul's words in Rom 12:1–2 offer a powerful foundation. He calls believers to "present your bodies a living and holy sacrifice," urging them to offer themselves wholly as an act of devotion. This isn't merely a ritual; it's what Paul describes as "spiritual worship"—a form of worship that is both thoughtful and deeply genuine, reflecting a willing commitment to God.

Paul goes on to draw a stark contrast between "do not be conformed" and "be transformed." Here, he emphasizes the necessity of an internal transformation, highlighting that spiritual maturity requires us to abandon worldly thinking patterns and instead embrace a continual renewal of our minds—a shift that aligns our thoughts with God's truth.

Paul explains that this renewal is essential to discerning and affirming God's will, which is defined by its goodness, acceptability, and completeness. Such transformation reflects the very essence of God's nature and his purpose for each of us. Paul's words invite us to see this renewal as not only a way of thinking but also a lifestyle that actively shapes our identity, our choices, and our worship.

This chapter delves into how believers can *renew their minds*, break free from limiting thought patterns, and fully embrace the perspective that God has designed for us.

HUMILITY, UNITY, AND LOVE IN ACTION

Paul's passage in Rom 12:3–21 encourages believers to cultivate a mindset of humility, unity, and love, which fosters a renewed mind and character aligned with God's kingdom.

Verses 3–8: Humility and Unity in Diversity

Paul begins by urging believers to think of themselves with "sober judgment," emphasizing that our self-perception should be grounded in humility and faith (v. 3). He then draws an analogy to the human body, illustrating how believers, though diverse in gifts, form one cohesive body in Christ (vv. 4–5). Each member has unique gifts—like prophecy, teaching, encouragement, and leadership—that serve the whole (vv. 6–8). This emphasis on humility and interdependence shifts focus from self-centered thinking to a perspective of mutual reliance and appreciation within Christ's body, helping believers see themselves and others through God's perspective.

Verses 9–13: Love and Service in Action

Paul highlights the importance of sincere love and dedication to what is good (vv. 9–10). This love is practical and selfless, characterized by zeal, patience, faithfulness in prayer, and generosity toward others, especially those in need (vv. 11–13). Such a mindset calls believers to reject superficiality and genuinely seek others' well-being. By focusing on sincere love and active service, believers are guided away from self-centeredness. Instead, they are encouraged to demonstrate God's love practically, leading to a renewed and spiritually mature outlook.

Verses 14–21: Responding to Opposition with Grace

Paul's guidance turns to how believers should respond to conflict and mistreatment: blessing rather than cursing, empathizing with others, seeking harmony, and avoiding pride (vv. 14–16). He instructs believers not to retaliate but instead to seek peace and leave justice to God (vv. 17–19). Paul's call to "overcome evil with good" (v. 21) reinforces a mindset that rises above personal vendettas and focuses on peace and forgiveness, allowing believers to respond to adversity with a transformed heart.

APPLICATION FOR RENEWING THE MIND

Paul's words in this passage do more than offer a general guide to personal growth—they ground believers in a communal context, highlighting how a transformed mind is essential to life within the Body of Christ. Through humility, love, and a focus on service, believers are called to renew their minds by embracing kingdom-centered values that benefit their personal walk and their relationship with others. These values—humility, unity, and forgiveness—create a life rooted in God's will, enhancing spiritual maturity and reflecting Christ to the world.

However, Paul's exhortation goes further, urging believers to apply these virtues within the faith community. He frames this transformation not as an isolated, individual experience but as an active, relational one meant to unify and strengthen the Body of Christ. This perspective aligns with his teaching about spiritual gifts, which are given for the benefit of others, emphasizing that renewed minds should drive believers to serve and support each other. This call to service may be particularly relevant within a local church setting but also extends to all members of the Body of Christ, shaping a believer's role as a contributing, nurturing part of the larger community.

By grounding our lives in these kingdom values, we grow spiritually and play an essential role in strengthening the Body of Christ. This kind of growth is not just for personal benefit; it builds up the unity and love within the church, which ultimately reflects God's kingdom.

Mark 10:43–45 captures this beautifully. Jesus tells us, "Whoever wants to become great among you must be your servant, and whoever wants to be first must be slave of all. For even the Son of Man did not come to be served, but to serve." This statement reveals that true maturity in Christ equips us not to lord over others but to serve humbly, following Jesus's example.

As we mature in our faith, we're being shaped to reflect God's love more deeply by serving others effectively. In this way, we live out our calling as members of his kingdom and as active ambassadors. By letting these truths guide our thoughts and actions, we live as Christ did, pouring into the lives of those around us and drawing others into God's kingdom.

Research supports the idea that serving others benefits mental, physical, emotional, and spiritual health in various ways. Serving others often intersects with spiritual and religious practices, offering coping resources that help reduce depression and anxiety while improving overall mental health and life satisfaction. This connection is especially pronounced among older adults and caregivers, who report increased life satisfaction and reduced burnout when they engage in service or receive support from spiritual beliefs.[8]

In addition to mental and emotional benefits, service-oriented and spiritual activities also correlate with improved physical health outcomes. People engaged in these practices often experience longer life expectancy, better pain management, and enhanced recovery from illness. Spirituality supports physical well-being by reducing stress and fostering resilience as part of a holistic health approach.[9]

On a spiritual level, acts of service are seen as inherently meaningful, deepening one's sense of purpose and meaning in life. This increased sense of purpose bolsters spiritual well-being,

---

8. Koenig and Cohen, *Link Between Religion and Health*.
9. Koenig et al., *Handbook of Religion and Health*.

which is closely tied to better mental health and enhanced emotional regulation, further contributing to an improved quality of life.[10]

Overall, the evidence consistently links serving others with positive impacts across mental, physical, emotional, and spiritual dimensions, suggesting that acts of service are an effective way to boost well-being by fostering resilience, life satisfaction, and a sense of purpose.

When we align our lives with the Kingdom of God, we invest in our minds' ongoing renewal. By choosing to live out kingdom values—love, peace, kindness, and humility—we are actively reshaping our perspectives and thoughts to reflect Christ's character. As Paul describes in Rom 12:2, this renewal process is crucial for growing in our identity as children of God.

As we dedicate ourselves to serving others and living with a kingdom mindset, we reinforce positive thought patterns and shed harmful ones that may hinder our growth. This investment in renewing our minds impacts every area of our lives, fostering a holistic well-being that extends beyond spiritual growth to improve our mental, physical, and social health. Engaging in meaningful service and community-oriented activities strengthens our relationships and contributes to greater resilience, peace, and a sense of purpose, helping us live fully as God intended.

UNDERSTANDING DISCIPLINE IN SCRIPTURE

I'm not particularly drawn to the concept of "spiritual disciplines" as they are often presented, primarily because many interpretations of these practices are heavily influenced by denominational views that, in my opinion, don't always align with Scripture. However, I see value in certain practices that I'll refer to as "disciplines," which can support our growth in faith.

---

10. Emmons and Crumpler, "Religion and Spirituality?," 731–44.

When we discuss *discipline* from Scripture, it's helpful to examine the Greek words used in the New Testament, which give us insight into what discipline really means.

The Greek term *paideia* is often translated as "discipline," but its meaning includes more than just correction. *Paideia* refers to the whole process of training, nurturing, and guiding, similar to how a parent might help a child grow and mature. It involves both encouragement and correction aimed at helping us grow. Hebrews 12:11 explains that, though discipline may seem challenging at first, it ultimately produces a "harvest of righteousness and peace" for those trained by it. This shows that God's discipline is ultimately about leading us toward a better, more mature character.

The second Greek term is *gymnazo*, meaning "to train" or "to exercise." Paul uses this word in 1 Tim 4:7-8, where he encourages Timothy to "train" himself for godliness. This word suggests self-discipline and effort, like an athlete's training to build strength. Just as athletes train consistently to reach their goals, spiritual growth also requires steady, disciplined practice.

Together, these words—*paideia* and *gymnazo*—provide a picture of biblical discipline. It's about balanced growth: receiving instruction and encouragement from God while also committing to active, focused practice. This balance of guidance and effort is what shapes us toward spiritual maturity.

STEPS FOR A RENEWED MIND: JOY, PRAYER, AND GRATITUDE

With this understanding of discipline, let's move into practical steps that can support a renewed mind. First Thessalonians 5:16-18 says, "Rejoice always, pray continually, give thanks in all circumstances." Paul's words here emphasize a life aligned with God's will through ongoing joy, prayer, and gratitude. Each of these actions is more than a single choice; they're enduring attitudes to adopt in all areas of life. Let's look at what each means.

Rejoice Always

"Rejoice" here speaks to a deep, lasting joy that doesn't depend on our circumstances. The Greek word *chairo* means to be glad, often in a way that arises from a state of grace or favor. Paul isn't asking us to be artificially happy; instead, he encourages a joy rooted in God's unchanging love for us. This joy persists because it's not tied to momentary experiences but to our relationship with God.

Think of it this way: rejoicing is about maintaining a hopeful outlook, knowing God is constant even when life isn't. It's not about ignoring difficulties but about seeing past them and remembering God's promises. This kind of joy changes how we react to challenges, helping us find strength and peace in God, no matter the circumstances.

Pray Continually

When Paul urges us to "pray continually," he's inviting us into a steady, ongoing conversation with God. The Greek term *proseuchomai* for "pray" suggests an active connection with God—a constant openness and ongoing communication rather than only praying at specific times.

This doesn't mean we have to kneel in formal prayer 24/7; instead, it implies keeping our hearts open to God at any moment. Continual prayer keeps us aligned with God, helping us seek his guidance, feel his presence, and rely on his strength as we go through each day.

Give Thanks in All Circumstances

Lastly, Paul calls us to "give thanks in all circumstances." This gratitude is more than feeling thankful for obvious blessings; it's about trusting God's goodness even when things are tough. In Greek, *eucharisteo* (to give thanks) suggests acknowledging God's grace. Paul challenges us to focus on what we can be grateful for, regardless of what's happening around us.

Practicing gratitude renews our minds by shifting our focus from what's lacking to what's been given. When we thank God for all things, we develop resilience and see each situation through the lens of faith.

In summary, Paul's advice to rejoice, pray, and give thanks shapes a way of life that keeps our hearts and minds connected to God's will. By letting these attitudes become part of our daily rhythms, we're better able to grow spiritually, deepen our resilience, and stay aligned with the peace and purpose God has for us. This is the kind of transformation Paul spoke about in Rom 12:2, where renewing our minds in these ways enables us to live in sync with God's intentions.

LIVING AS AMBASSADORS FOR CHRIST

With a renewed mind, we step into the role of ambassadors for Christ, representing his kingdom in a world that often follows different values. As his representatives, we bring the culture, love, and principles of God's kingdom into our everyday lives, carrying his message to those around us. This role is both a privilege and a calling that goes beyond personal growth—it's a mission that reflects God's character to the world.

As ambassadors, we embody the attitudes of service, peace, and humility that Christ modeled. When we're rooted in his values, our transformation speaks to others, showing them a glimpse of what life in God's kingdom looks like. This focus also contributes to our own well-being, aligning every part of our lives with God's design—our thoughts, actions, and relationships—shaped by his peace and purpose.

Our role as ambassadors is ongoing, influencing how we live in every environment—whether in our families, workplaces, or communities. With transformed minds, we demonstrate God's love, patience, and resilience, inviting others to see Christ through us. This commitment is part of our renewed life, drawing others to the kingdom through lives marked by grace and love.

CHAPTER 7 STUDY QUESTIONS

1. **A Life of Devotion and Transformation**: Reflect on Rom 12:1–2, where Paul calls us to present ourselves as living sacrifices and avoid conforming to worldly patterns. What does it mean to you to offer your life as "spiritual worship?" How can you make this a daily act of devotion?

2. **Humility, Unity, and Love in Action**: Paul emphasizes humility, unity, and love within the Body of Christ (Rom 12:3–21). How can you practice humility and contribute to unity in your community of believers? Which of Paul's teachings on love and service most challenges or inspires you?

3. **Breaking Free from Limiting Thought Patterns**: Are there specific thought patterns or perspectives you feel God calling you to change? How can you take practical steps to renew your mind and align your thoughts with God's truth?

4. **Responding to Conflict with Grace**: In Rom 12:14–21, Paul instructs believers to bless those who mistreat them and to overcome evil with good. Reflect on a time when you faced conflict or mistreatment. How could you respond in a way that reflects God's grace and peace?

5. **Developing a Renewed Mindset**: Paul speaks of transforming our minds by embracing humility, love, and kingdom values. In what ways do these values help you overcome self-centered thinking? How does adopting a kingdom mindset influence your personal growth and relationships?

6. **Practical Steps for a Renewed Mind**: In 1 Thess 5:16–18, Paul encourages rejoicing, continual prayer, and gratitude. Which of these do you find most challenging? What practical actions can you take this week to develop a mindset grounded in joy, prayer, and thankfulness?

7. **Living as Ambassadors for Christ**: With a renewed mind, we are called to represent Christ's kingdom. What does being an ambassador for Christ look like in your everyday life?

How can you reflect kingdom values—such as peace, humility, and love—in your interactions with others?

8. **Application of Kingdom Values**: How can you actively practice the values discussed in this chapter, such as service, humility, and unity? Think of specific actions you can take to embody these values in your community or relationships.

CHAPTER 8

The Gospel in a Digital Age

IN AN EVER-CHANGING CULTURE driven by the digital age, where communication evolves at blinding speeds, one truth remains unchanging: the gospel. God's message of love, redemption, and purpose hasn't shifted, even as the world around us becomes more complex and fast-paced. With screens, notifications, and endless streams of information vying for our attention, it's easy to get swept up and even subtly shaped by it all.

Yet, in the midst of this digital noise, we're called to maintain a kingdom mindset—one that grounds us in God's truth and keeps our focus on him. Technology has many benefits, but it also brings distractions, comparisons, and pressures that can pull us away from who we are in Christ. In this chapter, we'll explore practical ways to renew and guard our minds, stay anchored in our faith, and live out God's kingdom values in a world constantly on the move.

NAVIGATING DISTRACTIONS AND STAYING AUTHENTIC

Today's digital world brings unique challenges for Christians, especially as we live in a culture that's always "plugged in." Technology at our fingertips makes distraction a constant struggle, with endless notifications and information pulling us away from time with God and moments of quiet reflection. Social media adds its own set of pressures. It's easy to fall into a cycle of comparison, where our worth seems tied to likes, followers, or appearances. With so much focus on image, staying grounded in our true identity in Christ can be hard.

While technology connects us to more people than ever, these connections often lack the depth and honesty that real community requires. What was meant to bring us closer can sometimes leave us feeling more isolated and unfulfilled. Digital culture also tends to reward outward appearances, making it hard to live with the honesty and transparency that Christ calls us to. God's desire for genuine, vulnerable connection stands in sharp contrast to the polished image we often see online. Authenticity, not perfection, is what God seeks. By choosing to live authentically, we align with his purpose and stay connected to his truth rather than getting lost in a digital version of ourselves.

In a fast-paced world, finding rest and slowing down can be challenging. True Sabbath and times of disconnect are harder to come by, often robbing us of the restorative rhythms God intended for us. With everything moving at such a fast pace, it's difficult to engage deeply with Scripture, as we're increasingly conditioned to digest information in bite-sized pieces. Practicing habits like setting aside regular, focused time to reflect on God's Word or creating boundaries for screen use can help us engage more deeply with God and restore balance. Finding rest in God's presence is essential, especially in a culture that glorifies busyness.

The sheer volume of information we're exposed to daily requires discernment as we navigate messages that don't always align with God's truth. Constant exposure to ideas and values that don't reflect the kingdom can dull our spiritual awareness. In this quick-access culture, we're called to slow down, examine what truly nourishes our spirit, and cultivate qualities like patience, self-control, and gratitude.

As we read the Bible and explore the culture within its pages, we can't help but reflect on how to build and maintain a kingdom mindset amid today's fast-paced, digital world. This reflection often raises questions about how God's Word, written so long ago, applies to the complexities we face now. When God inspired the writing of the New Testament—and the Old, for that matter—did he foresee the specific challenges of a digital age?

To some, the Bible may feel "old" or distant from modern life, but this invites a deeper question: Did God not only foresee our modern-day world but also equip his Word with the timeless wisdom we'd need? The truth is that God exists outside of time, seeing all of human history at once. The challenges we are currently facing may be new to us, but they do not come as a surprise to him. He understands what we need to remain grounded, even in the rapidly changing digital landscape. Although these challenges may seem urgent and overwhelming, Scripture provides timeless wisdom that directly addresses the complexities of our digital age.

PROPHETIC INSIGHTS FOR A CONNECTED WORLD

Daniel's prophecy of iron mixed with clay and John's Revelation offer insights that resonate in today's age of technology and global connectivity. These passages are more than symbols—they guide us to consider the deeper spiritual realities of a world that's more connected yet increasingly fragile. As we navigate the digital age, these prophetic images remind us that even systems that appear strong are often underpinned by instability. By living with a kingdom focus, we can resist this instability and stay grounded in God's truth despite the pressures around us.

THE DIGITAL AGE AS IRON MIXED WITH CLAY

Daniel's vision of iron mixed with clay symbolizes a structure that looks strong but is inherently fragile. Our digital age could be much like this, reflecting strength mixed with instability (Dan 2:41–43). Technology has given us incredible connectivity and influence, yet it also brings weaknesses and divisions that make us vulnerable. Our reliance on digital infrastructure strengthens governments, economies, and global alliances, yet it's a fragile strength. Cyber threats, misinformation, and cultural divides create instability, leaving society vulnerable beneath the surface. Social media, for example, connects us, but it can also divide us, creating echo chambers that fuel conflict rather than unity. In this way, the digital age reflects the clay in Daniel's vision—something that looks strong but is ultimately unstable.

In a world that depends so heavily on technology, we see both iron and clay: strength mixed with fragility. This reminds us that human systems, no matter how advanced, can't offer the stability that only God's eternal kingdom provides. Daniel's vision points us to that unshakable kingdom—a kingdom that won't crumble but endures forever.

A WORLD UNDER CONTROL

Revelation foretells a time of global control, where buying and selling require a specific mark. Today, with digital currencies and biometric systems, we see how such control could impact our lives. However, as citizens of God's kingdom, we must remember that our true security comes not from this world or its systems but from God, who provides for us regardless of the restrictions around us.

A GLOBAL WITNESS AND INFLUENCE

John's vision describes two witnesses whose deaths are witnessed by every nation, tribe, and language. This vision, unimaginable in his time, is plausible now through global technology. It serves as a reminder of the power of media to shape our thoughts and reactions. Similarly, Revelation describes powers unifying their authority, a concept mirrored in today's global alliances that often promote values at odds with God's kingdom. For those anchored in Christ, this calls for discernment and a steadfast commitment to God's truth.

LIVING WITH INTEGRITY AND KINGDOM FOCUS

In light of Isa 33:15–17, we're given a powerful vision of living with integrity—a life grounded in righteousness and sincerity that counters the digital world's constant distractions. This passage serves as a standard and a promise, reminding us that God honors those who choose to walk with him, even when surrounded by a culture pushing in the opposite direction.

Isaiah opens with "[those] who walk righteously and speak what is right" (Isa 33:15), calling us to a life marked by authenticity. In a digital world where so much of what we see is curated or filtered, we're called to resist the pressure to present ourselves in ways that don't align with our true identity in Christ. Walking in righteousness means moving through our online and offline lives with a commitment to truth, allowing our words and actions to reflect who we are in God rather than what's popular or fleeting. Avoiding the trap of superficial connections and focusing on relationships grounded in love and sincerity can help us stay aligned with his truth.

GUARDING AGAINST COMPROMISE

The verse goes on to describe someone who "reject[s] gain from extortion and keep[s] their hands from accepting bribes" (Isa 33:15). This is a reminder to resist the lure of easy shortcuts or compromised integrity, especially in a digital age where success can seem like it depends on bending the truth for clicks, followers, or instant visibility. God calls us to a higher standard, where we refuse to participate in practices that undermine our witness or prioritize quick gains over lasting truth.

Isaiah further describes those who "stop their ears against plots of murder and shut their eyes against contemplating evil"

(Isa 33:15). In our culture, saturated with constant information and instant access to content of all kinds, this verse challenges us to be vigilant about what we allow into our minds and hearts. Guarding ourselves from harmful or toxic influences means consciously choosing to avoid content that glorifies violence, fear, or division. Instead, we are encouraged to seek out what is pure and true, choosing to be shaped by messages that build up rather than tear down.

SECURITY IN GOD'S PROMISE

As we choose to live in this way, Isaiah promises that "they are the ones who will dwell on the heights, whose refuge will be the mountain fortress. Their bread will be supplied, and water will not fail them" (Isa 33:16). Here, God assures us that a life of integrity, even in a world that pressures us to conform, is not only possible but is protected and provided for by him. Living with a kingdom mindset places us in a position of spiritual security, grounded in a foundation that won't shift with the changing currents of digital trends. God becomes our safe place, meeting our needs in ways that don't rely on the world's approval or validation.

FOCUSING ON THE ETERNAL KINGDOM

Finally, Isaiah closes with the beautiful promise that "your eyes will see the king in his beauty and view a land that stretches afar" (Isa 33:17). This reminds us that our ultimate focus is not on the temporary realities of this world but on the eternal Kingdom of God, where Jesus, our King, reigns. By keeping our hearts and minds set on him, we experience a glimpse of his beauty now, even as we look forward to the day when we will see him face-to-face.

A LIFE SET APART

In the context of our digital age, Isa 33:15–17 becomes a blueprint for a life that resists distraction and stays anchored in God's truth. It reminds us that our security, satisfaction, and ultimate purpose come from living with integrity and focusing on God's kingdom, not from the fleeting rewards of the world around us. In doing so, we find ourselves not only sustained by God but deeply rooted in the unshakable hope of his eternal kingdom.

PAUL'S CALL TO LIVE DIFFERENTLY

Paul echoes this call to a set-apart life in Eph 4:17, opening with a bold, emphatic statement urging believers to live differently from the world. He begins by saying, "So I tell you this, and insist on it in the Lord" (Eph 4:17), stressing that his teaching carries the authority of the Lord himself. This isn't just Paul's opinion; it's a directive from God. His message is clear: "You must no longer live as the Nations do" (author's paraphrase)—a call for a radical change in lifestyle for those who belong to Christ.

Paul then describes the way of life among the nations: "in the futility of their thinking" (Eph 4:17). Their thinking, Paul explains, is ultimately empty and purposeless, lacking the substance and direction that come from God's truth. He continues, "They are darkened in their understanding" (Eph 4:18), which suggests they're spiritually blind. Their understanding is clouded, preventing them from seeing clearly the things of God. Paul goes on to say that they are "separated from the life of God because of the ignorance that is in them" (Eph 4:18). This ignorance isn't just a lack of knowledge but a willful rejection of God's truth, and it leaves them alienated from the spiritual life God offers.

A HARDENED HEART AND LOST SENSITIVITY

Paul attributes this condition to "the hardening of their hearts" (Eph 4:18). Their hearts have become resistant to God's truth, insensitive and unresponsive to his guidance. This hardened state has led them to "[lose] all sensitivity" (Eph 4:19), meaning they're morally numb, no longer feeling guilt or conviction over their actions. Because of this, Paul explains that they have "given themselves over to sensuality" (Eph 4:19), willingly surrendering themselves to shameless indulgence in immoral behaviors.

In fact, Paul notes, they indulge in "every kind of impurity with greediness" (Eph 4:19, NASB). This phrase underscores the complete lack of boundaries in their actions—they engage in all forms of impurity, driven by an insatiable desire for more. Paul paints a vivid picture of a life marked by moral corruption and unchecked greed, a path that only pulls them further from God's truth and life. This description parallels Paul's words in Rom 1:18, where he speaks of those "who suppress the truth [of God] by their wickedness" (Rom 1:18).

A RENEWED LIFE IN CHRIST

In Eph 4:20-25, Paul shifts focus, reminding believers that the way of life they've learned in Christ is completely different from the world around them. He starts with an important contrast: "That, however, is not the way of life you learned when you heard about Christ and were taught in him in accordance with the truth that is in Jesus" (Eph 4:20-21). With this, Paul emphasizes that this new life is rooted in the truth of Jesus himself, not in the empty patterns of the past.

Paul goes on to describe what this change looks like. He says, "You were taught, with regard to your former way of life, to put off your old self, which is being corrupted by its deceitful desires" (Eph 4:22). The old self, he explains, is marked by desires rooted in deception—a lifestyle that's ultimately self-destructive. But this isn't just about rejecting past behaviors; it's about something deeper, a total transformation that starts in the mind.

Paul continues: "To be made new in the attitude of your minds" (Eph 4:23). This renewal is more than surface-level change; it's a shift in the core of our thinking, a realignment that happens as we learn to see and value life through God's perspective. With this renewal, we're called to "put on the new self, created to be like God in true righteousness and holiness" (Eph 4:24). The new self is not only different from the old but is designed to reflect God's character, embodying the qualities of integrity and purity that are grounded in truth.

Paul then gets practical, urging believers to "put off falsehood and speak truthfully to your neighbor, for we are all members of one body" (Eph 4:25). Here, he's not just giving a moral guideline but is pointing out that honesty is foundational to unity in the Body of Christ. Since we belong to each other in this new life, truth becomes essential to building genuine relationships within God's kingdom.

In a digital landscape where influences constantly vie for our attention, Paul's message serves as a reminder to live according to the deeper truth we've learned in Christ. His call to renewal challenges us to live transformed lives, grounded not in fleeting trends but in God's unchanging wisdom.

TRANSFORMED BY THE GOSPEL

In these verses, Paul clearly demonstrates the gospel's transformative power. He calls us to reject the old, corrupt ways and actively embrace a renewed mindset and life that aligns with God's truth. This life in Christ is a call to integrity, truth, and a commitment to reflect God's holiness in a world that often values the opposite.

GUARDING OUR MINDS WITH INTENTIONAL FOCUS

We must remember that what we allow into our minds shapes and controls our thoughts, attitudes, and actions. Therefore, it's crucial to take control of what we let in. A great starting point is to follow Paul's encouragement: "Finally, brothers and sisters, whatever is true, whatever is noble, whatever is right, whatever is pure, whatever is lovely, whatever is admirable—if anything is excellent or praiseworthy—think about such things" (Phil 4:8). The Greek word *logizesthe* (loh-GHEE-zes-theh), translated as "think," is an imperative command, underscoring the need to actively focus on or "logically dwell on" these qualities.

Now we return to the command, "Do not conform to the pattern of this world, but be transformed by the renewing of your mind. Then you will be able to test and approve what God's will is—his good, pleasing and perfect will" (Rom 12:2). Here, transformation refers to a *metamorphosis*, a profound change that comes through the renewing of our minds. This renewal happens only by controlling what we allow into it. Proverbs 4:23 reinforces this, saying, "Above all else, guard your heart, for everything you do flows from it." Likewise, Col 3:2 urges us to "set your minds on things above, not on earthly things." These are essential truths for anyone who seeks to live with a kingdom mindset, especially in the ever-changing landscape of the digital world we now navigate.

In a digital age that constantly vies for control over our beliefs, thoughts, and actions, guarding our hearts and minds is essential. Paul's words provide powerful guidance: "Do not be anxious about anything, but in every situation, by prayer and petition, with thanksgiving, present your requests to God. And the peace of God, which transcends all understanding, will guard your hearts and your minds in Christ Jesus" (Phil 4:6–7).

This isn't just advice; it's a life-altering approach. Instead of letting anxiety take root, we're called to bring every concern to God through prayer, anchored in thanksgiving. In doing so, we gain something profound: God's peace—a peace beyond any human understanding. This peace doesn't just comfort us; it actively guards our hearts and minds, keeping us grounded in Christ Jesus, even in a world that's constantly trying to shape us.

CONCLUSION

In a world increasingly shaped by digital influence, grounding ourselves in God's truth is essential. By focusing on what is true, noble, right, and praiseworthy, we align ourselves with God's eternal wisdom, empowering us to stand firm amidst the distractions of this digital age. Transformation through the renewing of our minds is not a one-time event but an ongoing pursuit that aligns us with God's will.

As we close this chapter, may we remember that our true fulfillment, purpose, and security are not found in the trends of this world but in the promises of God's kingdom. In every decision, every piece of information we consume, and each moment online, we have the chance to reflect his light—guarding our hearts and minds with discernment, integrity, and faith.

CHAPTER 8 STUDY QUESTIONS

1. **Maintaining a Kingdom Mindset in the Digital Age**: Reflect on the idea that God's Word, though written long ago, contains timeless wisdom that applies even in today's digital culture. How can you use Scripture to ground yourself in a kingdom mindset amid the fast-paced, ever-shifting digital world?

2. **Prophetic Insights for Today's Connected World**: Daniel's vision of iron mixed with clay in Dan 2:41–43 speaks to strength mixed with instability. In what ways do you see this reflected in today's digital age? How can you remain grounded in God's eternal kingdom amid the fragile systems of this world?

3. **Responding to Global Control and Influence**: Revelation mentions global control over buying and selling, which seems more plausible now with digital currencies and technology. How does knowing that your true security is in God affect your response to societal pressures or restrictions?

4. **Living with Integrity in a World of Distractions**: Isaiah 33:15–17 provides a vision of living with integrity and sincerity. How does this passage challenge you to walk righteously

and guard what you allow into your mind and heart in a digital culture that often values appearances over authenticity?

5. **Guarding Against Compromise**: What are some ways you can resist the temptation to compromise your values for quick gains or popularity, especially online? How can you protect your integrity and maintain a witness that aligns with God's truth?

6. **Focusing on the Eternal Kingdom**: Isaiah 33:17 describes a vision of seeing the King in his beauty, reminding us of our ultimate focus on God's eternal kingdom. How can this focus guide you in making choices that reflect eternal values rather than temporary digital trends?

7. **Living a Life Set Apart**: Paul's words in Eph 4:17–25 call us to live differently from the world. What practical steps can you take to reflect God's truth and live set apart, even in environments that may not support your faith?

8. **Guarding Your Mind with Intentional Focus**: Philippians 4:8 encourages believers to focus on what is true, noble, right, and praiseworthy. How can you apply this advice to guard your mind and avoid distractions that hinder spiritual growth?

9. **Finding Peace in a World of Anxiety**: Philippians 4:6–7 describes the peace of God that guards our hearts and minds in Christ. How can you practice bringing your concerns to God in prayer and experience this peace, especially in the digital age where anxiety can easily take root?

10. **Reflecting Kingdom Values in a Digital World**: How can you apply the values of love, peace, humility, and truth as you interact with others online and offline? Think of specific ways to let these values shape your choices and reflect God's kingdom in the digital landscape.

CHAPTER 9

The Unshakable Kingdom: Living with Hope and Purpose

A KINGDOM THAT WILL NOT FADE

TODAY, WE WATCH AS countless kingdoms and powers rise and fall, each one striving for control, yet all ultimately destined to fade away. Political systems come and go, cultural movements emerge and shift, and world powers grasp for influence—each leaving a temporary mark. But amid these passing kingdoms, there is one that is not built or sustained by human effort and that has already been set in motion: the kingdom Jesus brought into being. As Daniel foretold, "The God of heaven will set up a kingdom that will never be destroyed, nor will it be left to another people" (Dan 2:44). This kingdom doesn't simply coexist alongside earthly powers; it will ultimately bring them to an end. It is God's eternal kingdom—unshakable, enduring, and inviting us to live under its reign now, even as we look forward to its complete fulfillment.

REFLECTING ON OUR JOURNEY

In this chapter, we'll pause to reflect on the journey we've taken, touching on the key themes that have deepened our understanding of God's kingdom and how we fit into it. We'll briefly revisit what we've learned so far about kingdom identity, transformation, and the process of maturity. This reflection prepares us to consider the impact of God's kingdom in today's world. Even in a world that often opposes kingdom values, we see signs of God's reign advancing and his truth bearing fruit, showing us glimpses of his unending rule.

Finally, we'll look ahead to the ultimate fulfillment of God's kingdom. Scripture points to the day when Jesus will take all rule and authority from earthly kingdoms, establishing his throne over an everlasting kingdom that will never pass away. This vision of the future isn't just a distant hope—it's a call for each of us to respond now, to live out kingdom values in our daily lives, and to embrace our place as citizens of the eternal kingdom that one day will be fully revealed.

Throughout this journey, we've unpacked what it means to be part of something far greater than ourselves—a kingdom that stands apart from the values and priorities of this world. We began by exploring our identity as children of God, discovering that our true citizenship isn't tied to earthly systems but belongs to a kingdom marked by righteousness, peace, and joy. Flowing from this identity are the core beliefs that shape our actions, guiding us to live differently as ambassadors of God's eternal rule.

From there, we turned to the process of transformation and renewing the mind. We're not merely spectators of God's kingdom; we're transformed to live fully within it. By aligning our thoughts with God's truth, we're able to let go of old ways of thinking and embrace a new mindset that reflects the values of his kingdom. This transformation is essential, equipping us to live with purpose and conviction as his people.

But we know this journey isn't without its challenges. We face obstacles to spiritual growth—fear, distractions, and the pull of worldly desires—that can hold us back from maturing. Yet, as we press forward, we grow in our ability to overcome these distractions, grounding ourselves in God's kingdom and stepping more fully into who we are called to be. Overcoming these obstacles allows us to experience the depth of kingdom living, embracing the values and mission God has given us.

Finally, we've looked at what it means to live as citizens of God's kingdom right now. Though we live in a world filled with temporary powers and shifting values, we are called to follow an eternal standard. This means embodying the love, righteousness, and mercy of God's kingdom in our everyday lives. As citizens of a kingdom that will never fade, we are set apart from the world's values, staying grounded in the unchanging truth of God's reign.

LIVING AS CITIZENS IN THE PRESENT AGE

God's kingdom isn't something far off or only in the future; it's a reality here and now. After proclaiming that "the kingdom of God has come near" (Mark 1:15), Jesus set in motion a power that continues today. This kingdom is active, advancing in the world even as it faces opposition. We see God's love, righteousness, and mercy breaking through, often in places we might least expect.

In our present age, we see the signs of God's kingdom at work in transformed lives (2 Cor 5:17), in communities shaped by compassion, and in people who live out kingdom values with integrity and courage. Every act of love, every moment of grace and truth, reveals the presence of God's rule. Jesus said, "The Kingdom of God is within you" (Luke 17:21, NASB), showing that his kingdom is wherever lives are changed to reflect his love and righteousness.

Of course, this kingdom still meets resistance. Earthly powers and values stand opposed to God's rule, and we're called to live out kingdom values faithfully in this tension. Jesus reminded us, "In this world, you will have trouble," but also said, "Take heart! I have overcome the world" (John 16:33). Despite opposition, every act of love, every transformed life, and every choice to live by God's standards is a witness to his kingdom on earth.

As we live in this world, we're called to recognize and join in God's work, embracing our role as citizens of his kingdom right now. While it may seem subtle at times, God's kingdom is advancing—one life, one choice, and one act of faith at a time. Each day, we have the privilege of participating in his unfolding plan, living out the reality of his reign while holding fast to the hope of its full revelation (Phil 3:20–21).

As we look forward, we catch a glimpse of the day when Jesus will take full rule and authority over every earthly kingdom. This isn't just a distant hope; it's a guaranteed reality that Daniel prophesied long ago: "The God of heaven will set up a kingdom that will never be destroyed, nor will it be left to another people" (Dan 2:44). This eternal kingdom is a foundation we can depend on, unlike any fleeting empire or system. Knowing this gives purpose to living for God's kingdom here and now. The choices we make today, the values we live by, and our commitment to his truth aren't just for this moment—they echo into eternity as part of his unshakable plan.

After describing the coming destruction of the temple, Jesus's disciples asked him when these things would happen. Jesus outlined the events leading up to the end, concluding with this promise: "And this gospel of the kingdom will be preached in the whole world as a testimony to all nations, and then the end will come" (Matt 24:14). His words remind us that the message of God's kingdom will reach every corner of the earth, affirming that our lives and our witness contribute to something lasting—his kingdom that will one day be fully realized.

We also catch a powerful vision of God's kingdom fulfilled in the book of Revelation, where John describes scenes that reveal the ultimate triumph of God's reign. In Revelation, we see the moment when God's kingdom takes full control: "The seventh angel sounded his trumpet, and there were loud voices in heaven, which said, 'The kingdom of the world has become the kingdom of our Lord and of his Messiah, and he will reign forever and ever'" (Rev 11:15).

Later, John shares a vision of the new heaven and new earth, where everything broken is made new: "Then I saw 'a new heaven and a new earth,' for the first heaven and the first earth had passed away . . . And I heard a loud voice from the throne saying, 'Look! God's dwelling place is now among the people, and he will dwell with them. They will be his people, and God himself will be with them and be their God. "He will wipe every tear from their eyes. There will be no more death" or mourning or crying or pain, for the old order of things has passed away'" (Rev 21:1–4).

These visions remind us that God's kingdom is not only a present reality but a future certainty. We live in anticipation of this complete restoration, where God will dwell with his people, and every form of suffering will be wiped away.

THE QUESTION OF SUFFERING

This brings us to a question many who struggle with faith in Christ often ask yet rarely receive a satisfying answer for: "If there is a God, why is there so much evil and suffering in the world?" While fully addressing this would take more space than we have here and could fill entire volumes, I'll offer a brief response.

GOD'S PLAN OF RESTORATION THROUGH CHRIST

First, as we've been exploring throughout this book, God is a just and loving Creator who seeks to restore humanity to a right position and purpose within his design. Through his divine wisdom, God chose to bring about that restoration through Jesus Christ's work on the cross. Jesus ushered in God's kingdom, and by placing our faith in him, we are invited to become part of it. Scripture tells us that at the moment of genuine faith, we are made completely new—"holy and blameless in his sight" (Eph 1:4)—as though we had never strayed from his purpose. In this restored state, we stand fully redeemed and are welcomed into the kingdom God originally intended for us.

THE BATTLE AGAINST GOD'S DESIGN

Yet we know that God's purpose doesn't go unchallenged. Satan, the enemy of God, is committed to undermining his design and has set out to destroy his creation—especially us, whom God values deeply. Satan's primary weapon is deception, planting lies that people accept as truth. This began with his rebellion in heaven, continued with the temptation of Adam and Eve, and has affected humanity in every generation since. Jesus described Satan as "the father of lies" and said that "he was a murderer from the beginning, not holding to the truth, for there is no truth in him" (John 8:44). From the start, Satan's lies have been the driving force behind sin and suffering in the world, turning people away from God's design and bringing pain and separation.

A PURPOSE IN ALLOWING FREE WILL

God, in his sovereignty, could have chosen a different way to restore humanity—one that removed all evil completely. But to do so would have meant eliminating everything that had ever functioned outside his design, including humanity itself. Evil, at its core, is living outside of God's purpose. As Paul reminds us, "All have sinned and fall short of the glory of God" (Rom 3:23). If God had removed everything opposed to his purpose, there would have been no room left for us.

Instead, God's plan allows each of us the opportunity to turn to him in faith and be made new. As 2 Cor 5:17 says, "If anyone is in Christ, the new creation has come: The old has gone, the new is here!" Each person who responds to God has a unique place in his kingdom and has been prepared for good works (Eph 2:10). Yet not everyone who may ultimately respond to God has had the chance, and some have not yet been born. God, existing outside of time, knows every life and every choice. Ps 139:16 tells us, "Your eyes saw my unformed body; all the days ordained for me were written in your book before one of them came to be."

Even so, there is a time coming when God's kingdom will be fully revealed, and everything outside his design will be separated out. Jesus spoke of this in Matt 13:49-50, saying, "The angels will come and separate the wicked from the righteous and throw them into the blazing furnace." This will be the ultimate decision, where those who have chosen to reject Christ will face eternal separation from God's presence—a place the Bible describes as hell because it is without God's Spirit or life. Until that time, though, God allows humanity the freedom to choose. He is patient, "not wanting anyone to perish, but everyone to come to repentance" (2 Pet. 3:9). If he were to remove all who live outside his design right now, he would have to take away the very freedom that allows us to choose a relationship with him.

THE PURPOSE OF SUFFERING

So, why does God allow evil and suffering in the world? It's because suffering is a result of humanity's choice to live outside of God's design. To completely eliminate evil would mean cutting off the potential for all those who are still to believe. Instead, God allows time, patiently waiting for those who have yet to place their faith in him.

This is not to say that God is indifferent to the suffering or evil in the world. In fact, it deeply grieves his heart. Scripture shows us that God feels sorrow for the pain we experience. Through Ezekiel, he says, "I take no pleasure in the death of the wicked, but rather that they turn from their ways and live" (Ezek 33:11). God doesn't delight in pain or in the consequences of sin; like a compassionate Father, he is moved by the brokenness in his creation.

And not only does God see our suffering, but he also understands it. Through Jesus, God experienced pain firsthand. Isaiah describes Jesus as "a man of suffering, and familiar with pain" (Isa 53:3). And Heb 2:18 reminds us, "Because he himself suffered when he was tempted, he is able to help those who are being tempted." Jesus entered fully into our world of pain and sorrow. He doesn't stand apart from our struggles; instead, he stands with us, knowing our pain and walking with us through it all.

OUR PRESENT SUFFERINGS AND FUTURE GLORY

Paul gives us a profound way to view suffering, one that applies not only to the struggles in our own lives but also to the widespread suffering we see in the world around us. He writes, "I consider that our present sufferings are not worth comparing with the glory that will be revealed in us" (Rom 8:18). The pain, injustice, and brokenness we encounter, while deeply troubling, are ultimately temporary and will be overshadowed by the eternal glory God has promised. Paul invites us to see the suffering in our world through the lens of God's ultimate plan for redemption and restoration, a perspective that brings a sense of hope even amid our questions.

Paul further emphasizes that "the creation waits in eager expectation for the children of God to be revealed" and that all of creation "was subjected to frustration" but will one day "be liberated from its bondage to decay and brought into the freedom and glory of the children of God" (Rom 8:19-21). This passage reminds us that it's not only humanity that longs for redemption but all of creation itself. Every part of God's world, currently held in the grip of suffering and decay, waits for the fulfillment of God's promise. God's intention is to restore all things, bringing an end to suffering, pain, and brokenness on every level. One day, his glory will bring both humanity and creation out of suffering into complete restoration.

This hope we hold is not just wishful thinking; it's a confident expectation anchored in God's faithfulness. The promise of this coming transformation gives us perspective, reminding us that while suffering is real, it is not final. One day, everything will be made right as God's kingdom is fully revealed, bringing complete peace, justice, and restoration to all creation

THE COMING OF GOD'S KINGDOM

Building on this hope, Jesus constantly pointed to the coming of God's kingdom, speaking of both its current reality and its future fulfillment. Early on, Jesus declared, "The time has come . . . The kingdom of God has come near. Repent and believe the good news!" (Mark 1:15). In this simple yet powerful statement, he revealed that God's kingdom was already beginning to break into the world through his life and work. This was a call for people to turn from their old ways and believe, to join in what God was doing.

THE KINGDOM AMONG US

Jesus also spoke about the kingdom's presence among his followers. When the Pharisees pressed him to say when God's kingdom would come, he responded, "The Kingdom of God is not something that can be observed . . . because the Kingdom of God is in your midst" (Luke 17:20–21, NASB). With these words, Jesus pointed to a spiritual reality—a kingdom already present wherever hearts were turned toward God, even though it wasn't something that could be seen in a typical way.

THE PARABLE OF THE MUSTARD SEED

In one of his most well-known parables, Jesus compared the kingdom of heaven to a mustard seed, a tiny seed that grows into a large tree where birds can find refuge (Matt 13:31–32). Though the kingdom started small, Jesus assured us it would grow, providing life and shelter for many. This growth wasn't instantaneous, but over time, God's kingdom has become a transformative, life-giving reality in the world. And today, it has indeed grown into that large tree Jesus described, extending branches of hope and refuge for all who seek it.

A CALL TO ALIGN WITH GOD'S WILL

In the Lord's Prayer, Jesus taught us to pray, "Your kingdom come, your will be done, on earth as it is in heaven" (Matt 6:10). With this prayer, he showed us that God's kingdom is not just a distant hope but a present call to action, asking for God's will to become a lived reality in the here and now. It's a prayer that stirs us to align our lives with his purposes.

THE SPREAD OF THE GOSPEL AND THE KINGDOM'S FULFILLMENT

Jesus also linked the kingdom's final fulfillment to the spread of the gospel, saying, "This gospel of the kingdom will be preached in the whole world as a testimony to all nations, and then the end will come" (Matt 24:14). In other words, the reach of God's kingdom extends to all people, and the culmination of God's plan involves the world knowing his good news.

AN INHERITANCE OF ETERNAL KINGDOM

Finally, Jesus spoke of the kingdom as an inheritance prepared for those who live faithfully, promising that one day, the King will say, "Come, you who are blessed by my Father; take your inheritance, the kingdom prepared for you since the creation of the world" (Matt 25:34). This is the eternal, lasting kingdom we are invited into, one not bound by earthly rule but fully rooted in God's reign.

LIVING WITH ETERNAL PURPOSE

By painting this picture of God's kingdom—present and future—Jesus reminded us that we live for something eternal, something that makes every act of faithfulness worthwhile. His words invite us to step fully into God's kingdom here, confident in the promise of what is yet to come. With this understanding, we move forward, knowing each step we take today has a place in God's eternal kingdom.

LIVING AS CITIZENS OF AN UNSHAKABLE KINGDOM

As we journey through a world of shifting realities, we must hold fast to the truth that our lives are rooted in something far greater—God's kingdom, which is eternal and unmovable. While earthly powers rise and fall, and cultural values come and go, we are part of a kingdom established by God himself, a kingdom that will never fade. This eternal foundation calls us to live with purpose, knowing that we are grounded in a truth that endures beyond anything this world can offer.

Hebrews reminds us, "We are receiving a kingdom that cannot be shaken" (Heb 12:28). This assurance invites us to live lives of worship and reverence, knowing that we are part of something unshakable. In a world that often opposes kingdom values, we stand with the profound understanding that God's kingdom is not just a distant hope but a present reality—a kingdom built on love, justice, and truth, breaking into our world even now.

Jesus said, "My kingdom is not of this world" (John 18:36), pointing to a reign that transcends earthly systems and values. Living as citizens of this kingdom means living by its values—loving others, seeking justice, showing mercy, and walking humbly with our God (Mic 6:8). Each act of faith, each choice to live out God's truth, reflects the reality of his kingdom and points to what is both here and yet to come.

Paul encourages us to "set our minds on things above, not on earthly things" (Col 3:2), for our "citizenship is in heaven" (Phil 3:20). Our choices, priorities, and pursuits are no longer shaped by the temporary promises of this world but by the eternal truth of God's kingdom. Our lives carry eternal significance as we live out God's unfolding plan for redemption, stepping fully into our role as citizens of his kingdom.

We hold onto a sure hope, knowing that one day, God's kingdom will be fully revealed, and every form of suffering, pain, and brokenness will be wiped away. Revelation gives us a vision of this future when God's dwelling place will be with his people, and "he will wipe every tear from their eyes" (Rev 21:3-4). This promise fuels our commitment to live faithfully here and now, knowing that God's ultimate restoration is coming.

As citizens of this unshakable kingdom, we are called to be salt and light in the world (Matt 5:13-16), bearing God's love and truth into every circumstance. Every act of love, every choice to walk in faith, echoes into eternity, reflecting the kingdom we belong to and bearing witness to God's unchanging reign. Though we may face challenges, we stand secure, knowing that we belong to a kingdom that will stand forever.

So, as we live in a world of temporary things, may we stand with courage, carrying the values of God's eternal kingdom within us. His reign is unending, and in that truth, we find the hope, strength, and purpose to live as faithful citizens of his kingdom.

CONCLUSION

In this chapter, we explored what it means to live as citizens of God's unshakable kingdom. Grounded in a truth that endures beyond the shifting values and fleeting powers of this world, we are part of an eternal kingdom established by God himself—a kingdom that is both present and yet to be fully realized. Living out this reality calls us to align our choices, values, and purpose with the kingdom of heaven, embodying love, justice, mercy, and humility as Jesus taught.

We are reminded that while our lives are rooted in heaven's citizenship, we have a vital role here on earth. Our commitment to kingdom living reflects the stability and hope of God's reign, even in the midst of a world that often resists these values. Paul encourages us to fix our minds on things above, and as we do, each act of faith, each moment we choose to walk in kingdom truth, bears witness to the eternal purpose we carry.

Looking forward, we hold onto the promise of God's final restoration, when every trace of pain and brokenness will be erased, and God will dwell fully with his people. Until that day, we live as salt and light, letting the reality of his kingdom shine through our lives, anchored in the unchanging hope of his rule and reign.

CHAPTER 9 STUDY QUESTIONS

1. **A Kingdom That Will Not Fade**: In what ways does the temporary nature of earthly powers contrast with the eternal nature of God's kingdom, as described in Dan 2:44? How does this truth impact the way you view your role and purpose in God's unshakable kingdom?

2. **Reflecting on Our Journey**: Reflect on your understanding of kingdom identity, transformation, and maturity. How has this journey through the book shaped your view of yourself as a citizen of God's kingdom and your role in today's world?

3. **Living as Citizens in the Present Age**: Jesus proclaimed that "The kingdom of God has come near" (Mark 1:15). How do you see God's kingdom at work in the world today? What are some specific ways you can live out kingdom values, even when they may be at odds with worldly influences?

4. **The Reality of Resistance**: In John 16:33, Jesus acknowledged that we would face trouble but also assured us of his victory. How does this promise help you navigate the tension between living kingdom values and facing opposition? How can this hope encourage you in moments of difficulty?

5. **Participating in God's Unfolding Plan**: Philippians 3:20–21 reminds us that our citizenship is in heaven. What does this heavenly citizenship mean to you, and how does it shape your daily choices, values, and priorities as a part of God's kingdom?

6. **Looking Forward to the Fulfillment of God's kingdom**: Daniel 2:44 and Rev 11:15 describe God's ultimate rule over all earthly kingdoms. How does this vision of the future impact your sense of hope and purpose as you live out your faith today?

7. **The Question of Suffering**: Many wonder why God allows suffering. Reflect on the reasons provided in this chapter, particularly God's patience and desire for all to come to repentance (2 Pet 3:9). How does this understanding shape your response to suffering and your faith in God's justice and love?

8. **Living with Eternal Purpose**: Jesus taught us to pray for God's kingdom to come and his will to be done (Matt 6:10). How does this prayer challenge you to align your life with God's eternal purposes? What specific actions can you take to reflect his kingdom in your daily life?

9. **The Promise of Restoration**: Revelation 21:3-4 provides a vision of God's future kingdom where all suffering will be erased. How does this promise give you hope in the present, and how can it influence the way you interact with others as you share God's love and truth?

10. **Embracing Our Role as Citizens of an Unshakable Kingdom**: Hebrews 12:28 calls us to live in reverence as part of God's unshakable kingdom. What steps can you take to carry the values of this eternal kingdom with courage and faithfulness in a world filled with temporary distractions?

CHAPTER 10

Embracing the Kingdom Life

As we come to the end of this journey, we're reminded that the message of the kingdom is not merely an idea to study but a truth to live out. The gospel of the kingdom calls us to step into a new reality, one where our identity, purpose, and future are transformed by Christ. We're invited not just to know about the kingdom but to experience it in every part of our lives.

This life is about more than rules or obligations—it's about becoming who we were meant to be. Through every chapter, we've explored the foundational truths of God's kingdom: from the good news of salvation, the transforming power of faith and repentance, to the call to live with purpose as citizens and ambassadors of God's reign. Each of these principles isn't just knowledge to hold in our minds; it's an invitation to real, active faith that changes us from the inside out.

Paul, in his letter to the Romans, reminds us of the simplicity and depth of this calling: "Confess with your mouth that Jesus is Lord and believe in your heart that God raised him from the dead, and you will be saved" (Rom 10:9, NASB). This is the doorway into God's kingdom—not by our own effort, but by faith. When we confess and believe, we are adopted into God's final kingdom, heirs to a throne that cannot be shaken. As his children, we belong to the kingdom that will stand forever—a kingdom built on love, justice, and truth, where we are secure in our Father's promises.

Embracing the Kingdom Life

Living as citizens of God's unshakable kingdom means allowing the values of heaven to shape how we think, speak, and act. It's choosing to walk in love, humility, and truth even when the world around us promotes self-interest, pride, and compromise. It's aligning our hearts with God's character, letting his Spirit renew our minds daily so that we reflect the light of Christ in a world that desperately needs him.

The path to spiritual maturity may have obstacles, but as we've learned, we have the Holy Spirit's strength and God's armor to stand firm. God calls us to grow in faith, to deepen our love for him, and to serve others with the same grace we've been given. As heirs of his promises, we live not just for today but with a hope rooted in eternity—a hope that strengthens us and fuels our purpose.

Now, the question is this: will we choose to live out the kingdom life wholeheartedly? Each of us has a role to play, a unique purpose crafted by God to advance his kingdom here and now. Our daily lives, our choices, our relationships—each one is an opportunity to reflect his truth and his love.

As you go forward, remember that you are a citizen of "the Last Kingdom"—God's eternal and unshakable kingdom. Stand firm in that truth, letting it guide you through every season, every challenge, and every joy. Pursue the life of this kingdom with all your heart, knowing that God's promises are sure and his presence goes with you. In each step you take and every choice you make, may you bear witness to "the Last Kingdom," God's final, unbreakable reign that will endure forever.

CHAPTER 10 STUDY QUESTIONS

1. **Experiencing the Kingdom Life**: Reflect on the idea that the Kingdom of God is not just something to know about but a truth to live out. How can you actively incorporate kingdom values into every part of your life? What changes might this call you to make?

2. **A New Identity and Purpose in Christ**: Throughout this book, we've explored the transformation that comes with embracing our identity as children of God. How has this journey shaped your understanding of who you are in Christ? How does this identity influence your purpose and direction in life?

3. **Living by Faith**: Romans 10:9 emphasizes that confessing Jesus as Lord and believing in his resurrection is the doorway into God's kingdom. How does this simple yet profound statement impact your understanding of faith and salvation? What does it mean for you to live each day by faith in God's promises?

4. **Citizenship in God's Unshakable Kingdom**: As citizens of an eternal kingdom, we are called to live with integrity, love, and humility. How can you align your thoughts, words, and actions with the values of God's kingdom, even when they contrast with worldly values?

5. **Reflecting God's Character**: We are invited to let God's Spirit renew our minds so that we reflect Christ's light in the world. In what areas of your life do you feel called to grow in love, humility, or truth? How can you let God's character shine through you?

6. **Overcoming Obstacles to Spiritual Maturity**: This book has highlighted various challenges to spiritual growth. What obstacles do you encounter most often, and how can you rely on the Holy Spirit's strength and God's armor to overcome them?

7. **Embracing Your Role in God's Kingdom**: Each of us has a unique purpose in advancing God's kingdom. What specific role or calling do you feel God has placed on your heart? How can you live this out in your daily interactions and relationships?

8. **Living with Eternal Hope and Purpose**: As heirs of God's promises, we live with a hope rooted in eternity. How does

this eternal perspective influence your purpose and choices? In what ways can you bring God's hope to those around you?

9. **A Commitment to the Kingdom Life**: The final call of this chapter asks if we will choose to live the kingdom life wholeheartedly. What does a wholehearted commitment to God's kingdom look like for you? What practical steps can you take to pursue this commitment each day?

10. **Bearing Witness to The Last Kingdom**: Reflect on what it means to be a citizen of "the Last Kingdom"—God's final, unshakable kingdom. How can you stand firm in this truth through various seasons of life, and in what ways can you witness to God's eternal reign in the world around you?

Glossary of Key Terms

Abiding in Christ: Living in ongoing connection with Jesus, allowing His presence to shape and guide every aspect of our lives, remaining faithful and grounded in Him (Jn 15:4-5).

Adoption: The act through which God brings believers into His family, giving them the status of sons and daughters with full inheritance rights in His kingdom, motivated by His kindness and love, not obligation (Eph 1:5).

Atonement: Jesus' sacrificial death that reconciles believers to God by imparting His righteousness to them. Through the atonement, believers stand in Christ's righteousness, are restored to a relationship with God, and are adopted into His kingdom (Rom 3:25; 2 Cor 5:18).

Blessings: Gifts from God, both spiritual and material, which empower believers to fulfill His purpose. Spiritual blessings particularly refer to the resources and strength we receive in Christ (Eph 1:3).

Body of Christ: A term for the church, describing all believers who, though diverse in gifts and backgrounds, form a unified and interdependent community under Jesus as the head (1 Cor 12:27).

Glossary of Key Terms

Born Again: The spiritual rebirth that occurs when a person places faith in Jesus, marking the start of a new life, free from the bondage of sin and alive in the Spirit (Jn 3:3).

Calling: God's specific purpose for each believer, aligning their lives with His kingdom values and mission, empowering them to serve and represent His kingdom (Eph 4:1).

Confession: Recognizing and admitting one's sins to God, which leads to forgiveness and healing. It also refers to openly declaring faith in Jesus, affirming allegiance to His kingdom (1 Jn 1:9; Rom 10:9–10).

Covenant: A binding promise between God and humanity, established on God's faithfulness. The New Covenant through Jesus offers forgiveness and a new relationship with God (Heb 9:15).

Discipleship: The process of following Jesus, learning from His teachings, and allowing His Spirit to transform one's life, leading to growth in Christlikeness (Mt 28:19–20).

Eternal Life: The abundant and unending life that begins with faith in Jesus and continues forever, marked by a close relationship with God and participation in His kingdom (Jn 3:16).

Faith: Trust in God's promises, particularly in Jesus' work on the cross. Faith is active and leads to actions aligned with God's will, transforming the believer's life (Heb 11:1).

Flesh: The human tendency toward sin and opposition to God's Spirit. Living "according to the flesh" involves selfish desires that conflict with God's kingdom (Gal 5:17–21).

Fruit of the Spirit: The qualities produced in a believer's life through the Holy Spirit, including love, joy, and peace. These fruits reflect God's character (Gal 5:22–23).

Glossary of Key Terms

Gospel: The good news of Jesus Christ, which declares that God's kingdom has come, offers forgiveness and new life, and invites people to follow Jesus (Mk 1:15; 1 Cor 15:1–4).

Grace: God's generous and unearned favor, through which He saves, transforms, and sustains believers in a relationship with Him (Eph 2:8–9).

Holiness: Being set apart for God, marked by purity and obedience. Holiness reflects God's nature and is His purpose for each believer (1 Pet 1:15–16).

Holy Spirit: The third Person of the Trinity, who empowers, guides, and transforms believers, equipping them for kingdom life and ministry (Jn 14:26).

Idolatry: Placing anything or anyone above God in one's life. Idolatry can take many forms, from material possessions to personal ambitions (Ex 20:3–5).

Justification: Being declared righteous by God through faith in Jesus, which restores the believer's relationship with God and assures them of forgiveness (Rom 5:1).

Kingdom of God: God's reign, both present and future. It's not limited to a location but encompasses God's rule and presence wherever His will is done (Lk 17:21).

Law and Gospel: The law reveals God's standards and our need for salvation; the gospel brings the good news of Jesus, who fulfills the law on our behalf (Rom 8:3–4).

Mercy: God's compassionate forgiveness extended to humanity despite their sins, reflecting His love and desire to restore us (Lam 3:22–23).

Glossary of Key Terms

New Creation: The transformed identity of a believer in Christ, marked by a departure from the old, sinful nature and embracing a new life aligned with God (2 Cor 5:17).

Peace of God: The inner calm that comes from trusting in God, surpassing understanding, and guarding one's heart and mind in Christ (Phil 4:7).

Prayer: Communing with God through praise, confession, thanksgiving, and requests. Prayer is essential for growth and alignment with God's will (Mt 6:9–13).

Propitiation: God's proactive grace in dealing with sin, not to satisfy wrath but to restore relationship through Jesus' sacrificial love. The term *hilasmos* reflects God's active mercy, not anger (1 Jn 4:10).

Redemption: Liberation from sin's bondage through Jesus' sacrifice. Redemption frees and restores believers to live as God's children, fully aligned with His purpose (Eph 1:7; Ps 103:12).

Repentance: Turning from sin to realign with God's design and purpose, leading to transformation and restored relationship (Acts 3:19).

Righteousness: Being morally right in God's eyes, achieved through faith in Jesus and reflected in a life that honors God (Mt 5:6).

Salvation: Deliverance through the power of the gospel, bringing freedom from sin, renewal, and restoration in relationship with God (Rom 10:9–10).

Sanctification: The ongoing process of becoming more like Christ, marked by growth in holiness and spiritual maturity (1 Thess 4:3).

Glossary of Key Terms

Sin: Any action, thought, or behavior contrary to God's design, leading to separation from Him and reflecting a life outside His purpose (Rom 3:23).

Spiritual Maturity: Growing in faith and Christlikeness, reflecting a deeper understanding and commitment to God's kingdom (Eph 4:13–15).

Transformation: The deep change brought by the Holy Spirit, aligning one's thoughts, desires, and actions with God's will (2 Cor 5:17).

Truth: God's reality, fully embodied in Jesus. Truth is the foundation of a believer's life and must guide their thoughts and actions (Jn 14:6).

Unity of the Body: The harmony among believers, who are all members of Christ's body, called to love, serve, and grow together (Eph 4:3).

Wisdom: Understanding and applying God's truth in practical ways that honor Him and benefit others (Jas 1:5).

Worship: Honoring God through a lifestyle of reverence, gratitude, and obedience, which goes beyond rituals and reflects true devotion (Rom 12:1).

Bibliography

Alford, Henry. *Alford's Greek Testament: An Exegetical and Critical Commentary* 2. 8 vols. Grand Rapids: Guardian, 1976.

Brown, Raymond E., and John P. Meier. *Antioch and Rome*. Mahwah, NJ: Paulist, 1983.

Emmons, Robert A., and Cheryl A. Crumpler. "Religion and Spirituality?: The Roles of Sanctification and the Concept of God." *Journal of Social Issues* 61.4 (2005) 731–44.

George, Linda K., and David B. Larson. "Religious Influences on Physical Health." In *Handbook of Religion and Mental Health*, edited by Harold G. Koenig et al., 191–201. San Diego: Academic, 1998.

Hudders, L., and M. Pandelaere. "The Silver Lining of Materialism: The Impact of Luxury Consumption on Subjective Well-Being." *Journal of Happiness Studies* 13.3 (2012) 411–37. https://consensus.app/papers/silver-lining-materialism-impact-luxury-consumption-hudders/36cbd6cb501b5346931e5bb930ccf54f.

Johnson, Luke Timothy. *Among the Gentiles: Greco-Roman Religion and Christianity*. New Haven, CT: Yale University Press, 2009. https://consensus.app/papers/among-gentiles-grecoroman-religion-christianity-johnson/b5fd6cdb51ea5ae7acc3adcc469a51c2.

Kittel, Gerhard, and Gerhard Friedrich, eds. *Theological Dictionary of the New Testament*. Translated by Geoffrey W. Bromiley. 10 vols. Grand Rapids: Eerdmans, 1964–76.

Koenig, Harold G., et al. *Handbook of Religion and Health*. 2nd ed. New York: Oxford University Press, 2012.

Koenig, Harold G., and Harvey J. Cohen, eds. *The Link Between Religion and Health: Psychoneuroimmunology and the Faith Factor*. New York: Oxford University Press, 2002.

Krause, Neal, and R. David Hayward. "Religious Involvement, Practical Wisdom, and the Development of a Sense of Meaning in Later Life." *The Journals of Gerontology: Series B* 69.2 (2014) 185–94.

Lampe, Peter. "Social Welfare in the Greco-Roman World as a Background for Early Christian Practice." *Acta Theologica* 23 suppl. 1 (2016) 1–28. https://

consensus.app/papers/social-welfare-grecoroman-world-background-christian-lampe/4eca8d3066ec5b27b239bf8a2589e1dc.
Landers, R. "Review of *Consuming Religion: Christian Faith and Practice in a Consumer Culture*, by Vincent J. Miller. New York: Continuum, 2003." *Choice Reviews* (2007). https://doi.org/10.5860/choice.42-0241a.
Miller, Vincent J. *Consuming Religion: Christian Faith and Practice in a Consumer Culture*. New York: Continuum, 2003.
Moo, Douglas J. *The Epistle to the Romans*. Grand Rapids: Eerdmans, 1996.
Packer, J. I. *Knowing God*. Downers Grove, IL: InterVarsity, 1973.
Pargament, Kenneth I., and Julie J. Exline. *Working with Spiritual Struggles in Psychotherapy: From Research to Practice*. New York: Guilford, 2021.
Scheidel, Walter. "A Peculiar Institution?: Greco–Roman Monogamy in Global Context." *The History of the Family* 14.3 (2009) 280–91. https://consensus.app/papers/institution-greco-roman-monogamy-context-scheidel/310ab40211db57d7ab00e6a3684da7f3.
Strong, James. *Strong's Exhaustive Concordance of the Bible*. Nashville, TN: Thomas Nelson, 1890.
Thayer, Joseph H. *Thayer's Greek-English Lexicon of the New Testament*. Peabody, MA: Hendrickson, 1889.

www.ingramcontent.com/pod-product-compliance
Lightning Source LLC
Chambersburg PA
CBHW070509090426
42735CB00012B/2712